Sta. Clara Co. Library   APR 13 '89

CA   P9-EDT-703   NA

Santa Clara
County
Free Library

REFERENCE

 58 1 6

Sta. Clara Co. Library
CENTRAL REFERENCE   APR 13 '89

Mission La Concepcion
Purisima

FOR BEHOLD FROM HENCEFORTH ALL NATIONS SHALL CALL ME BLESSED.
—*St. Luke, 1:18*

A WOMAN CLOTHED WITH THE SUN, AND THE MOON UNDER HER FEET,
AND ON HER HEAD A CROWN OF TWELVE STARS.

Apoc. XII:I.

New Series. Local History

Mission La Concepcion Purisima

DE MARIA SANTISIMA

BY

Fr. ZEPHYRIN ENGELHARDT, O. F. M.

*Author of "The Missions and Missionaries," "The Franciscans
in Arizona," "Mission Dolores," "Mission San
Diego," "Mission Santa Barbara,"
"Mission San Gabriel," etc., etc.*

*"Colligite quae superaverunt fragmenta,
ne pereant," John, vi, 12.*

McNally & Loftin, Publishers

1986

Santa Barbara

SANTA CLARA COUNTY LIBRARY

3 3305 22004 8841

Imprimi Potest,

FR. NOVATUS BENZING, O. F. M.,
Minister Provincialis

Nihil Obstat,

M. F. WINNE, C. M.,
Censor Deputatus

Imprimatur,

JOHN CAWLEY, Vicar General
July 14, 1932.

Original Copyright © 1932
by
Zephyrin Engelhardt O.F.M.

McNally & Loftin, Publishers
and
Prelado de los Tesoros
La Purisima Mission State Historic Park

Printed at Kimberly Press, Inc.
Goleta, California

Library of Congress Cataloging-in-Publication Data

Engelhardt, Zephyrin, 1851-1934.
Mission La Concepción Purísma de María Santísima.

(Missions and missionaries of California. New series, Local history)
Reprint. Originally published: 1932.
Includes index.
1. Mission La Purísima Concepción (Calif.)—History. 2. Franciscans—
Missions—California—History. 3. California—History—To 1846. 4.
California—Church history.
I. Title. II. Series.
F869.M65E54   1986   282'.79491   86-18076
ISBN 0-87461-066-4
ISBN 0-87461-067-2 (pbk.)

Reissue Preface

For decades, this volume of Fr. Zephyrin Engelhardt's series of sixteen histories of the twenty-one California missions has rarely been available in bookstores. In spite of some criticism that the famous historian writes from a standpoint biased in favor of the mission programs, his books on the missions and missionaries of early California are still the most complete and authentic accounts of these historic institutions. Fr. Engelhardt (1851-1934) was Archivist at the Santa Barbara Mission where the Archive-Library contains the largest collection of documentary material on the California missions to be found anywhere.

As a primary source for information on La Purisima Mission, located three miles northeast of the City of Lompoc and seven miles southeast of Vandenberg Air Force Base in Santa Barbara County, this chronicle is unsurpassed. Because the mission is in a pastoral setting fifteen miles west of U.S. 101, it is not visited by tourists as often as most of the other missions. This relatively unspoiled isolation enhances its appeal.

Its acquisition by the State Department of Parks and Recreation and its accurate reconstruction in the 1930's by the Civilian Conservation Corps earn its reputation as one of the most interesting State Historical Parks in California. Fascinating interpretations are provided by the highly competent, dedicated and well-informed Park staff and Prelado de los Tesoros, the volunteer docent organization. They insure that a visitor to this mission will leave with a better understanding and appreciation of the role of the missions in California history.

Richard S. Whitehead
July 14, 1986

PREFACE

Mission Purisima occupies a unique position on the western coast of America, in as much as it was the first Mission Establishment dedicated to the honor of God, under the complete title: "The Immaculate Conception of the Blessed Virgin Mary."

It is remarkable that this dedication took place long before the Immaculate Conception was declared a dogma of Faith and prior to the request of the American hierarchy to the Holy See for Mary, as Patroness of the United States, under the same title.

For six hundred years, Mary Immaculate has been honored by the Franciscan Order as its chief Patroness. We are therefore happy to record that further proof of this Franciscan affection has been given by the Very Reverend Father Provincial, Novatus Benzing, O. F. M., who, in the name of the Province of Santa Barbara, has generously supplied the funds required for the publication of this book.

Owing to the illness of the author, the details of the printing of this work, were supervised by the assistant historian, Fr. Felix Pudlowski, O. F. M.

The Author gratefully acknowledges himself indebted to Brother Matthew, O. F. M., for reading the printed proofs, and to Brother Gerald for typing the manuscript.

THE AUTHOR

CONTENTS

CHAPTER I.

CHAPTER II.

CHAPTER III.

CHAPTER IV.

CHAPTER V.

Contents

CHAPTER XI.

CHAPTER XII.

APPENDIX

ILLUSTRATIONS

SECOND MILITARY DISTRICT
III
PURISIMA MISSION
(1787-1840)

CHAPTER I.

Mission Purisima Concepcion, like Mission Santa Barbara, was contemplated many years before it could be established. The delay was due to the same influence that prevented Santa Barbara Mission from being founded—the animosity of Governor Felipe de Neve who, despite the royal regulations, did not want the missionaries to teach the savages mechanical arts, agriculture, and the raising of live stock. Since without these aids the Indians could not be induced to adopt Christianity, much less persevere in it, the Fathers refused to lend themselves to any scheme that did not include the civilization of the natives. The Missionary College of San Fernando de Mexico, which supplied the missionaries for California, through its Guardian and Councillors insisted that the system of conversion introduced from the beginning must be continued, or no more missionaries would be sent to the coast, as it would be useless to attempt the conversion of such a low class of people, as the Indians of California proved themselves, in any other way than the one that had showed such happy results. When the viceroy, therefore, urged the founding of more Missions on the Santa Barbara Channel, Fr. Francisco Pangua, Superior of the College, replied under date of December 18, 1780: "In order to establish the two Missions of Purisima Concepcion and Santa Barbara on the Channel, there are needed the same aids that the predecessors of Your Excellency have supplied for the founding of the Missions of San Diego, San Gabriel, and the others in that new territory as far up as the port of San Francisco, and which assistance is described in the accompanying invoice which I herewith present." After pointing out the goods needed for the church, the house, and the field at each Mission, for clothing, beads, and other little things with which to attract the Gentiles to the Christian Faith, the Fr. Guardian continues:

"All is necessary, Your Excellency, the things for the church as a matter of course; for what good purpose would it serve to instruct and baptize the heathen Indians, if thereafter it be not obligatory upon them to live and die as Christians? This cannot be done without the church building, bells, vestments, etc. The aid for the house and field is indispensable for the same reason, because, if they do not sow grain useful and necessary for human sustenance, the Missions will have little or no basis. For this same end all the implements and tools are likewise needed, and at least one blacksmith's forge to repair and renew the tools. Besides this, there is wanted for the Mission a sufficient number of cattle and all kinds of animals, even chickens, in order that in time the Missions may develop into pueblos proper . . . Likewise it is necessary that one year's stipends for the religious, who are to be put in charge of the Missions, be paid in advance so that they may take along whatever is needed during the first year. . . . for we have not wherewith to procure anything. The viceroy finally yielded, and directed the Missions to be founded in accordance with the wishes of the College and of the friars in California.[1] Thereafter the $1,000 required for establishing a new Mission and for providing it with the goods for church, house, and field, were allowed to be taken from the Pious Fund in charge of the Government, not from the royal treasury, although the pious fiction that a Mission was established at the expense of the king is noted in the title page of every Mission, perhaps at the request of the same Government.

When all obstacles had at last been cleared away, preparations were made for placing the Mission in a suitable locality. As early as March 24, 1786, even before the site of Mission Santa Barbara had been definitely chosen, Commandante General José Antonio Rengel, who had succeeded Neve, wrote to Governor Pedro Fages: "In your official

---

[1] *Missions and Missionaries of California*, vol. ii, pp. 371-381.

communication of June, 1785, you inform me that, after having surveyed the Channel of Santa Barbara scrupulously for the purpose of locating the Mission of Concepcion in accordance with the dispositions of the Reglamento, you have not found a place more to the purpose for its suitable proportions than that of Gaviota, which in addition affords a saving of ten to twelve leagues of road to the presidio. In consequence of this information, I direct you to proceed to found the said Mission: but first you will make another examination of the said place of Gaviota and of the other localities in its vicinity in order to assure yourself thoroughly of their advantages. After you have determined that there are no better places, and have convinced yourself to that effect, you will give me an account thereof so that Mexico may be petitioned to send the thousand dollars which the Reglamento assigns for the temporal aid of each of the new Missions that may be established."

Governor Fages transmitted this welcome news to the Fr. Presidente of the Missions, Fr. Fermin de Lasuén, on August 9, 1786, with the following remarks: "I forward this to Your Reverence for your information, and in order that I might be able to repeat the survey of the Rio de Santa Rosa (Santa Inés) which is the locality, not that of Gaviota, which by mistake is named in the forgoing order. The Mission may then be established in the coming spring and Your Reverence, if it pleases you, may accompany me so that the site, where the Mission should be located, may be chosen entirely in accord with Your Reverence's pleasure."

In reply Fr. Lasuén from Mission Santa Clara wrote under date of August 12, 1786: "I render to Your Honor every thanksgiving due to such noble attentions, and I shall at the first notification comply punctually with Your Honor's wishes in this particular."[2]

No details are extant regarding the second survey and the immediate preparations that were made down to the actual

---

[2] *Santa Barbara Mission Archives*, ad annum.

founding of the Mission, and this in Fr. Lasuén's hand is related on the title page of the baptismal register as follows:

"VIVA JESUS"[3]

"Book I of Baptisms of the Mission of the Most Pure Conception of the Most Holy Virgin Mary, Mother of God, and Our Lady, which was founded in the plain of the Rio Santa Rosa,[4] on the site called by its natives, *Algsacupi*, at the expense[5] of the Catholic King of Spain, Don Carlos III, (God protect him), by the Religious of the Apostolic College of the Propagation of the Faith of San Fernando de Mexico, to whom his Majesty confided the Conversion and the Administration of this whole new California. It was commenced on the happy day dedicated to the singularly Most Pure Mystery of the Empress of the Heavens, Mary Most Holy, that is to say of her *Immaculate Conception*, esto es de su Concepcion Inmaculada,[6] Saturday the 8th of the month of December, 1787. On this day I, the undersigned Presidente of these Missions, blessed water and with it the place and a large Cross, which we venerated and planted. I immediately celebrated the first holy Mass and preached, and we recited the Litany of All Saints. On the following day, Sunday, I said holy Mass, and in company with the governor I retired to Santa Barbara until the waters should subside. In the middle of March (1788) came the troops assigned to guard this post, and the servants for the purpose of erecting some shelter; and in the beginning of April, I came with the goods necessary for the founding, and with the two missionaries whom I had named as first founders,

---

[3] Blessed be Jesus!

[4] So named by the first expedition on August 30, 1769. See *The Missions*, vol. ii, pp. 38, 664.

[5] Only in the sense that the king *allowed* the money to be taken from the Pious Fund of California established for such purposes. See *The Missions*, vol. i. pp. 456-457; 593-599; vol. ii, p. 247.

[6] Under this title the Franciscans had venerated the Blessed Virgin as their Patroness for centuries, but it was not declared a dogma of Catholic Faith till December 8, 1854.

the Rev. Fathers Fr. Vicente Fustér of the Holy Province of Aragon, and Fr. Joseph Arroita of the Holy Province of Cantabria.

"This book consists of 276 pages for use, not counting the first and the last, which remain without numbers.

"In witness whereof, I have signed on April 10th, 1788.— Fr. Fermin Francisco de Lasuén.

"On the fly leaf, as was his custom at all the Missions, Fr. Commissary Prefect Vicente de Sarría, noted his Auto-de-Visita along with Fr. Estévan Tápis, the secretary of the visitation, on September 18, 1813; and again with Fr. Antonio Rodríguez as secretary on June 27, 1816.

The heading to the page on which the entries begin reads thus:

J. M. J.

"In the Name of the Most Holy Trinity, Father, Son, and Holy Ghost, of Our Lord Jesus Christ, and of His Most Holy Mother Mary, Our Lady, conceived without original sin in the first instant of her natural being. Amen."

The first entry records the Baptism of an Indian on April 9, 1788, who appeared to be *in articulo mortis* at the rancheria of Tajauchu or Santa Rosa. The convert was 22 years of age, a native of the rancheria of Sipuc, and named Matisaquit. He was given the name Francisco de la Concepcion by Fr. Arroita, who officiated. The Indian did not die at the time, however, for Fr. Fustér notes that on November 30, 1788, he supplied the ceremonies of necessity omitted by Fr. Arroita.

The first Baptisms administered in the church edifice, occurred on the eve of Pentecost Sunday, May 10, 1788. The converts were three adult Indians over twenty years of age, named respectively Mariano, Miguel, and José Maria; and three adult female Indians over thirty years of age, named respectively Maria Concepcion, Maria Rosa, and Ana Maria. In addition, on the same occasion two children were baptized —Juan Bautista and Clara.

The first native marriage was blessed by Fr. Fustér on

May 10, 1788. The happy couple were Mariano and Maria Concepcion, baptized on the same day, as mentioned in the preceding paragraph.

At the end of the first year of the Mission's existence, 1788, the Fathers had entered ninety-five Baptisms and twenty-five marriages, but no deaths. The first burial entered in the burial register was that of Juana de la Cruz, a child of an Indian neophyte couple, on February 14, 1789.

Building activities began in the spring of 1788. The Mission had been formally founded on December 8, 1787, and on the next day, too, holy Mass was celebrated on the spot by Fr. Lasuén in a brushwood shelter, as was usually the case; but rains had rendered it inexpedient to erect any other structures. There are no reports extant for the first years about building operations, but doubtless a chapel and a dwelling for the two missionaries was the first work undertaken in that line. Quarters for the guards followed, and, as converts rapidly entered the fold, cabins had to be put up for them. Shops and corrals arose in their turn as needed, all of adobes, doubtless, like the other structures.

Meanwhile Fr. Vicente Fustér, toward the end of August, 1789, returned to Mission San Juan Capistrano, and Fr. Cristóbal Orámas replaced him till November, 1792. Fr. José Antonio Calzada succeeding him.

The first official reports regarding building activities carried on at Purisima Concepcion are dated December 31, 1794, and signed by Fathers Arroita and Calzada. According to them, during the year 1794 new quarters for the soldier guards had been erected. The building measured 14 varas (about 38 feet) in length and 6 varas (about 17 feet) in width.

A warehouse for various goods and implements was next constructed; but the dimensions are not stated. A room 8 varas long for the officials, and a room for the outfits of pack animals, etc., 6 varas long, all of adobe and roofed with tiles, followed in succession. Lastly a corridor of brick was added to the main building.

In 1795 a vaulted granary 7 varas long, and contiguous to it another room 7 varas long were built. Both were roofed with tiles. In this year also the Fathers began to collect material for a new church.

During the year 1796 three capacious apartments were constructed for keeping implements and other things, and various structures were repaired or renovated.

THE THREE FRANCISCAN MISSIONS, SANTA BARBARA, SANTA INÉS, AND PURISIMA, IN SANTA BARBARA COUNTY.

In 1797 more suitable habitations were put up for the missionaries, but the dimensions have not been reported. In this year, too, Governor Diego Borica recommended to the Fathers a certain Antonio Henriquez as master weaver. On May 27, 1797, Fr. Gregório Fernández, who had succeeded to the management of the Mission after the departure of

Fathers Arroita and Calzada in the summer of 1796, replied as follows: "My very dear Señor:—On May 4th we received from Your Honor a communication dated April 29, in which you inform us that you have new orders from his Excellency (viceroy of Mexico) regarding the master weaver Antonio Henriquez. We have considered that, according to such orders, said artisan can be most useful at this presídio (Santa Barbara) for the public good, and perhaps also for the royal treasury. Availing ourselves of the generosity of Your Honor, we have cheerfully accepted the favor, which Your Honor has offered to us, by retaining him at this Mission for some days to oversee what little there is on account of the poverty of these new subjects of his Majesty, in order to decrease the expenses of the royal treasury."[7]

The last clause is significant. The experience at other Missions told the friars that the neophytes received little benefit from the instructions of the artisans, not to speak of other drawbacks. The Fathers were expected to pay the salary of the master weaver. In fact, Borica, on the same April 29, 1797, wrote that, in accordance with the order of the viceroy, the Mission would have to pay Henriquez twelve reales ($1.50) a day, or return him to Monterey.[8] Yet the missionaries were in the service of the king, as well as the soldiers at the presidio or at the Missions, and were transforming the savages into orderly subjects, all without expense to the government.

For the year 1798 the Fathers report the erection of a guardhouse for the soldiers. They also had nine houses built for as many convert Indian families, and another storehouse. All these structures were of adobe and roofed with tiles. On the same occasion, December 31, 1798, Fathers Gregório Fernández and Antonio Calzada write, as evidence of their poverty: "In the Biennial Report for 1793-1794, it was noted that from the founding of this Mission there have been lacking

---

[7] California Archives, Provincial State Papers Benicia, vol. xxv, p. 381.
[8] Cal. Arch., Prov. Records vol. vi, p. 660; Prov. St. Pap. Benicia, vol. xxv, pp. 379-380.

three copes—one each of red, green, and violet color, the canopy, and the processional Cross, for which reason, there being only one white and one black cope, the administration of the Sacraments and the other ecclesiastical functions were not performed or not celebrated with the solemnity and decorum commanded by our holy Mother Church. A large bell, which had come with the first church goods, is already broken.

"There are now 920 souls here, and the number, it is hoped, will be much greater with the favor of God. As the primitive church is not spacious enough to gather in it all the Indians and give them the spiritual food necessary, the missionaries here have seen themselves compelled to lay the foundations for the new church this year; but, owing to the entire ignorance of the Fathers, there is necessary a master or masters, who are experienced in this matter, otherwise the work will not be done with sufficient security for stability: but we also know not whence their pay shall come.—The Christian Doctrine is recited twice every day, the people assembling at the sound of the bell. The boys and girls, each class separately, are assembled for the instruction a third time.—The chief branches of industry so far are the weaving of cotton into cloth, and of the wool into blankets etc. Shoes, too, are already made at the Mission."[9]

For the last year of the century, 1799, the Fathers reported the construction of two buildings, or additions to the main building, each ten varas long. Both were built of adobes and roofed with tiles.

---

[9] *Report of December 31, 1798.*

CHAPTER II.

False Accusations Answered.—Fathers Exonerated.—Accuser Removed.
—Mission Activities.—Life at the Missions.—Building Activities.
—New Church.—Fr. Payeras Has News.—An Aqueduct.—Fathers
Wearing Shoes on Account of Cold Climate.

Little is known about the happenings, the successes and
reverses, at Purisima Concepcion Mission, nor about the hopes
and fears, the joys and sorrows of the missionaries. Here as
elsewhere the Fathers confined themselves to reporting briefly
just what was commanded by the Government and by the
Missionary College of San Fernando. At the beginning of the
new century, however, they were driven out of their beloved
retirement and forced into public notice through the accusations which one of the friars, who had gone insane at Mission
San Miguel, and who had therefore been returned to Mexico,
secretly made to the viceroy against the California missionaries. The viceroy, thereupon, directed Governor Borica to
institute a close investigation. The governor accordingly instructed the military commanders of the four presidios to
investigate unknown to the missionaries. For that purpose he
transmitted fifteen questions. The replies were communicated
to the viceroy, who in turn notified the Fr. Guardian of the
College. The latter requested Fr. Presidente Lasuén to have
the Fathers make full reports about the situation in the re-
spective Missions. Only the report of the comandante of the
presidio at Santa Barbara, Felipe de Goycoechea, reflected
seriously on the management of the Missions of Santa Barbara
and Purisima Concepcion. Fr. Lasuén forwarded the fifteen
questions and the reply thereto of Goycoechea to the Fathers
of the two Missions with the request that they report truth-
fully on every question of the governor. Although the complaints amazed and pained the missionaries, we are thankful
for the sake of history that the attack on the Fathers was
made, for it led to an official statement regarding the life at
the Missions, and the difficulties encountered by the devoted
friars, which would otherwise not have come to our knowledge.
Furthermore, it showed how disinterestedly the Fathers

labored and toiled, and how little recognition they received from the military authorities. The replies caused the removal of Goycoechea: and the viceroy moreover declared that the missionaries were entirely exonerated.[1] On account of the historical value and interest of the document, the replies to the fifteen questions are reproduced entire. The reader will, from the answers, easily infer the nature of the questions and of the accusations also, which are omitted for brevity's sake.

"Questions sent by the Governor of California, Don Diego de Borica, to the Comandantes, and the Replies of the Fathers of Mission Purisima.

1. The Christian Doctrine is taught to the Indians in Spanish and Indian.

2. Before baptizing them, the converts are instructed, as far as possible and according to their capacity, in the principal mysteries of our holy Religion, not exactly eight, ten, nor twelve days, but for as many days as are necessary.

3. We Fathers speak Castilian, and we endeavor to have the neophytes learn and speak it. They also speak their own language. We Fathers, soldiers, and Indians converse together in another jargon, a mixture of Mexican, Otomite, Lipan, Apache, Comanche, etc., which is commonly in use among the troops.

4. The Indians are not permitted to rove outside the Mission, or in the mountains, except for a limited time.

5. No neophytes have been rebaptized, because we Fathers take special care to know where the Indians reside who were baptized *in articulo mortis* outside the Mission, as well as the children of Gentiles who were baptized at the Mission. Furthermore we have these Gentile parents present such children in the hope that we Fathers will give them something when they come.

6. Every morning and evening the neophytes are given for their meals atole,[2] and pozole[3] for the mid-day meal, in

---

[1] For details on the subject, see *The Missions*, vol. ii, pp. 548-598.

[2] Gruel of corn meal.

[3] Porridge or thick soup of vegetables and meat.

sufficient quantity for their maintenance, without considering how little they labor generally, and without considering the frequent permissions that are granted them to collect wild seeds in season which are calculated to take up almost half the year; nor do we consider the wheat which is given in addition on Sundays and some other feast days, when there is distributed to each one almost half a peck. Moreover, during this year one hundred and ninety-four head of cattle have been slaughtered for them and sixteen cattle have been sold to the troops, although, according to the report of the past year, the herd of cattle consisted of only 400 head.

7. For clothing, the neophytes are given a woolen blanket and suit of cotton cloth, which if treated with some care will last more than a year, even a year and a half. In addition the men are given two breech cloths of Puebla woolen cloth or of cloth woven at the Mission. The women and girls receive gowns and skirts, and a blanket like the men.

8. The habitations of the Indians are the same to which they were accustomed in the pagan state, because until now it has not been possible to provide more convenient lodgings. The construction of the necessary buildings for the storing of the crops and for keeping other goods left no time for it. The apartment for the single women is a room fourteen yards square. Almost all around the walls inside are the bunks constructed of good boards, a little more than five palms from the floor, and proportionately wide. There they spread their mats and sleep very comfortably. In the same apartment they have a convenient place for their necessities. During the day they are not obliged to stay within, nor in any other apartment, unless it be as punishment for some misdeed. The single men, after they have recited the prayers near the apartments of the Fathers, are free to retire to their homes, or to the *pozolera*,[4] or they may remain to sleep in the corridors, which like the pozolera is outside the cloister.

---

[4] Pozolera, place where the meals were cooked, and afforded warmth for a long time during the night which might be very cold.

9. The number of hours alloted to the Indians for labor does not exceed five, and on most days they work scarcely four hours. There is no obligation to labor just so much and so long, except at such jobs that require piece-work: but that kind of work is proportioned with prudence and in no way is it increased, as has been done many a time at the presidios for the Indians hired from the Missions.—Pregnant, nursing, and aged women, and children are not engaged at more work than is necessary to keep the Fathers informed that they are at the Mission, for unless this be observed, they would not stay at the Mission, and the consequence would be that many of the aged would die in the mountains without the Sacraments of Penance and Extreme Unction, and the recently born would die without Baptism, as has happened many times.

10. The neophytes are permitted all kinds of diversions which are popular among them. Likewise half the year, or almost one-half of the year is granted them for gathering their wild seeds, in the various seasons.

11. Not only are the neophytes permitted to deal with the white people, but they are taught how to deal with them. They are given permission to approach the guards, and the soldiers are allowed the services for their chores whenever they ask, although many times the Indians are overburdened with work by the soldiers, or deprived of the fire and rest which those enjoy who labor at the Mission. The Indians then tell us that they do not want to go to work for the soldiers, but that they want to labor with the rest of the Indians. In such cases the Indians are allowed their choice and their freedom. They are punished if they leave the Mission furtively, especially at night, because then they forsake their wives, or because experience had taught us that such excursions have very bad results, for they solicit and lead away women, or steal, or do other things opposed to good order.

12. The punishments, which we apply to the Indians, of both sexes, are whipping, sometimes shackles, very seldom stocks, and also the lock-up. The misdeeds for which we Fathers chastize the Indians thus are concubinage, theft, and

running away. When the transgressions are against the common good, like killing cattle, sheep, or firing pastures, which has occurred sometimes, the corporal of the guard is notified.

13. In the ordinary sales, and at the prices fixed by the *arancel* (pricelist issued by the governor), we strictly adhere to the arancel, and we go beyond it only when the goods are larger or of superior quality. For instance, a soldier wants a yearling calf at the price of 12 reales ($1.50), but having put it in the corral for him it grows to one of 16 or 18 months; or he asks for a regular heifer, but leaves it to feed until it becomes a cow. Both these cases have happened at the Mission of San Luis Obispo with regard to the soldier Dolores Pico, who was transferred from Monterey to Santa Barbara. Fr. Fernandez goes on to cite various instances at some length, which are not important enough to reproduce. They merely show that the soldiers and the officers tried to outwit the Fathers in such deals, at the expense of the Indian community.

14. We Fathers do not provide ourselves with any other effects than those that come to us from Mexico. Sometimes we avail ourselves of the goods in the presidio storehouse. This was in answer to the question whether the Fathers procured for themselves wine or brandy in addition to the quantity sent them from Mexico by way of San Blas at excessive prices.

15. The balance of the account of this Mission in Mexico, according to the reports of this year, is $900, and a little more. The funds at hand in the Mission consist of about $160 due us from insolvent parties, but the presidio storekeeper for just reasons will recognize these dues; furthermore, over $30 worth of cigars, more than $16 worth of soap, eight or ten old, decrepit, inserviceable horses, which cannot be obtained from the debtors in payment of their debts. With some means collected there have been purchased four or five middling good horses. Then there is on hand in cash about $120. Let it be well understood that the money which circulates among the troops of Santa Barbara presidio is in the shape of soap and cigars. The same must be said of that of Monterey. Thus the soldier Agustin Marquez in order to pay for some cavalry

MISSION PURISIMA, WHEN FLOURISHING AT ITS SECOND SITE.

outfit, which he secured at this Mission, he had recourse to the comandante of Monterey, and what he gave him was $6 worth of cigars, with this he paid for the weapons.—Mission of Purisima Concepcion, December, 1800.—Fr. Gregório Fernandez."[5]

Returning to the narrative on the building operations, we have to note that in the year 1800 another wing was erected of adobe and roofed with tiles. This row measured 70 varas, or 190 feet in length, and seven varas or about 19 feet in width, and was divided into eight rooms.

For 1801 no reports are extant, but the new church must have been under construction, although the Fathers do not mention it once in connection with the building activities. They must have informed Fr. Presidente Lasuén, however, for in his Biennial Report of the years 1800-1802, he writes under date of February 21, 1803: "In the Missions of Purisima Concepcion and San Luis Rey they have in each one completed their church of adobe, sufficiently large and very becoming." That is all we find recorded anywhere about the church, the ruins of which are still seen on the southern end of Lompoc at the foot of the mountain, within three blocks of the Catholic church. We may presume that the dedication ceremonies took place on the titular feast, December 8, 1802, and that the Fathers of Santa Barbara Mission, as well as those of San Luis Obispo, participated in the festivities. During 1802, the garden, which measured about 200 yards square was surrounded with a single adobe wall.

We have no particulars about 1803, but in 1804 a guard-house and five dwellings, with as many kitchens, presumably one for each soldier and family, were built. These included a good patio. The whole structure was 40 yards long.

For the years 1805-1809 we have no details; but a personal letter of Fr. Mariano Payéras, who arrived late in 1804, dated May 8, 1808, and addressed to Fr. Presidente Estévan Tápis, explains what was done during these years. "The aqueduct

---

[5] *Santa Barbara Archives*, ad annum.

(zanja) was at last finished," he writes. It is no less necessary here than that in the Arroyo Seco at Soledad. It has come out better than I imagined. The great olive is on the level with the water, whence your Reverence will see that all the lands of Purisima are under irrigation. Those that do not secure water from above will have it from the river, which has water at least for the grains of the winter.

The same efforts have been made at Salsipuedes by collecting and damming the water of that arroyo. As all this has been effected in April, it has not been utilized fully, but in the future it will be a different matter. The crops promise at least a sufficient harvest for this year. 2,000 head of cattle have been incorporated with those which the Mission already had. All these efforts proceed from the pain it gives me to see these poor people in want, and from the strong desire to provide them with all the abundance this locality permits.

"Your Reverence knows this climate very well. Some say that it has changed greatly. The evidence which they give, together with what I have observed, make me believe that now it is more foggy and colder than ever. Hence Your Reverence will not wonder to see us wearing shoes, and always clad as necessity demands.—My Fr. Geronimo is well, and we both salute Your Reverence. Your least brother and servant, who kisses your hand, Fr. Mariano Payéras."

Fr. Tápis on the margin wrote: "I replied on May 12. I give permission that they may wear shoes and such clothing (underwear) as they know to be necessary for the preservation of health."[6]

In 1810, the report says that at the Rancho de San Antonio the necessary buildings were put up for those who had to live there and also a granary for the products expected was erected there.

An extremely interesting item is contained in the annual report for the year 1810. Fathers Payéras and Boscana write under date of January 1, 1811: "In order to facilitate travel

---

[6] *Santa Barbara Archives*, ad annum.

for the public and the mail carriers, and to shorten the road from Mission Santa Inés to this one, and from this Mission to that of San Luis Obispo, also on account of the many advantages which would evidently result to our community, two roads have been opened through the mountain of this river, one league apart and each forty paces wide."

The Fathers, notably Fr. Payéras, were certainly on the alert for the welfare of both Indians and colonists. The missionaries, of course, were extremely solicitous to procure the goods requisite for the church and sacristy, even though they appeared to be engrossed in the temporal welfare of their converts. However, the reports on the subject have been lost for the years preceding the year 1811. The goods for the church, house, and field formerly secured in Mexico with the stipends of the missionaries and in exchange for hides and tallow from the Missions, ceased with the year 1811. Thereafter the Fathers had to procure such goods, especially for the church, with donations received from colonists or in exchange for products of the Mission from merchants who happened to land at Santa Barbara or Monterey. In 1810 only a silver altar bread box, and two canvas paintings were obtained. In 1811 the reports add only one chasuble of variegated silk, with broad galloons of gold enamel.

CHAPTER III.

Missionary Changes at Purisima Concepcion.—The Missionaries not
Eager for Publicity.—Fr. Mariano Payéras' Most Interesting
Letter to Fr. Estévan Tápis.—The Longest Communication on
Personal Matters in the History of California.

During the first decade of the nineteenth century several
changes occurred in the management of the Mission. Fr.
Gregório Fernández served till about October 1805, and then
retired to the College of Mexico. Fr. Calzada, now always
ailing, was transferred to Mission Santa Inés in 1804. He was
succeeded near the end of the year by Fr. Mariano Payéras,
who in the following year became the senior missionary, having
since October, 1805, Fr. Juan Cabot as companion missionary.
The latter in December, 1806, was succeeded by Fr. Gerónimo
Boscana, who continued with Fr. Payéras till May, 1811.
This will explain some things in a special report of Fr. Payéras.
It is less an official report than a personal description of the
situation and of the incidents that occurred during his administration. Besides being the longest communication of its
kind extant between two missionaries in the field, the writer
a subject and the recipient a sympathetic Superior, it reveals
the heart that speaks at a time when there was no regulation de-
manding such information, and therefore more liable to appeal
to the sympathetic readers. Unfortunately, the missionaries in
California, owing to their manifold duties, and from indifference, too, confined themselves to rendering the annual accounts
prescribed by the Spanish Government or by the ecclesiastical
authorities. Hence, we have exact figures, indeed, but little
that concerns the personal experiences of the unselfish, spiritual
and temporal guides of the neophyte Indians, such as are
handed down in the *Literas Edificantes* of the Jesuit Fathers
in Lower California. Yet, the lives of the Franciscans in
Upper California must have been replete with incidents of an
edifying nature. In the following letter of Fr. Payéras we
shall find some specimens.

On January 13, 1810, Fr. Mariano Payéras wrote from
Mission Purisima to Fr. Presidente Estévan Tápis as follows:

"My Venerable Prelate-—A year has already passed since I wrote to Your Reverence. This was not for lack of affection, but because during this interval not the least incident occurred that might move me thereto, for which I rejoice and give a thousand thanks to God. The Annual Report which my companion, Fr. Gerónimo (Boscana) is remitting to you, will show you the state of the Mission. Nevertheless I shall not neglect to add to it by explaining more at length where it might be necessary. I commence with the spiritual affairs.

"I believe I have written to Your Reverence in these past years, that with the help of interpreters I compiled a large catechism with the acts of Faith, Hope, and Charity, and another with what is necessary for salvation, a complete *confesionario* (a booklet explaining all about confession), and other little things, all in the language of these natives. By dint of effective patience, we succeeded in having nearly all the men learn by heart the large catechism, and the very aged the little one. With the women, because after all they are women, teaching the catechism did not proceed so well. Those who already know the said number of prayers in their own language learn it in perfect Castilian, which costs them hard labor, because they are even greater blunderers than I. Many (even aged ones) have made their confession in Lent, and some have also received holy Communion.

"Since I came to the territory, wherever I have resided, I have not ceased to go about acquainting myself of the conditions at a Mission. Everywhere I have inquired, asked, etc., and now I must sincerely confess in the interest of truth that never have I believed that there would be among the Indians any error in Faith; but here I have encountered traces and signs of superstitions, witchcraft, and even idolatry. God is witness that I have endeavored in season and out of season, (but always with gentleness) to eradicate them by substituting for their extravagant ceremonies and worship of their Achup, the worship and adoration of the true God; but as in the case of the earth which is so overgrown with weeds, although it has not ceased to bear fruit, so it is clear what prudence and caution the wise and prudent missionary must observe in dealing with the said subjects of Confession and Communion.

"What beyond measure has exercised our patience in this year, and has grieved us deeply, is to see that the majority of the pregnant women have produced still-born babes. There have been weeks when there were two and three cases, strangely enough on the part of the youngest of the women. In the beginning it was attributed to the inconveniences of child-bearing. In order to prevent such occurrences, steps were taken to instruct them and to preach to them, and sometimes to punish them suitably; but down to the present time all this has been in vain. At the same time we have not been able to discover the origin and motive of such deplorable happenings.

"Your Reverence is not unaware of the fact that in this region paganism has ceased. The only adult baptized this year is the mother of Estévan Machado, whom it was possible to baptize in casil, where because of her great age she remained. The few pagans who show themselves, although it is announced to them, the Gospel avails them not, because their homes, according to information, are distant 25 to 30 leagues. Considering such a great distance it would perhaps not be expedient to baptize them (I am speaking for myself alone) without consulting both governments (i. e. the secular and ecclesiastical authorities).

"Sickness, although not so stubborn as in previous years, nor so continuous, is not lacking. In November last, one healthy adult fell dead while at work, and another on the following day scarcely obtained Extreme Unction. Among so many little troubles which annoy us every day, the natural tranquillity and docility of these poor Indians serve us as a balm; for they do not as much as long to visit the mountain regions. Then it is a consolation to see the affection and cheerfulness with which they apply themselves to whatever is assigned them; to hear them pray, sing (this year another Mass appeared which is very nice and full of music), and play

like musicians, sing like experts, and what crowns it all, to
see the greatest patience in their infirmities, the anxiety with
which even the very aged ones at the end of their life ask to
make their confession, and how most of them die with all the
sentiments and signs of a true and good Catholic. Let us
therefore rejoice in the Lord, and let us regard as well employed
whatever hardship, and let us continue with more firmness
and fervor to labor in this vineyard, hoping, that when Heaven
blesses our work, we shall every day gather more and more
abundantly the best fruit. Be it so.

"I now take up temporal matters. In no way do I want to
defraud my predecessors of all that merit and glory of which
their temporal and spiritual toils and labors at this Mission
have made them creditors. They did what they could and
knew; and they knew and did much. Your Reverence more
than I saw them and observed them; but in view of how I
found the Mission, and actually see it, I must give the most
grateful thanks to God, because I know He has poured out
His blessing without we meriting it, and in a manner we have
not comprehended. The maintenance in plenty of more than
a thousand souls, in a region so dry, that in five years scarcely
a grain has been raised due to rain, is not a little puzzling.
However, during the same time aqueducts have been dug
which promise abundant water for irrigation. Furthermore
new land has been cleared, all irrigable and within sight.

"Now the chance for sowing in the place which belonged to
Reyes happens to appear. When in January last I found that
the wheat sown was spoiled, not growing for lack of humidity,
the river dry, Salsipuedes even without a drop of water, and
the heavens harder than bronze, despairing of securing grain
for the mill, I had a council with the old men. I asked, and
after much talk I learned, that at Reyes there used to be a
little water. I flew thither at once, and I was agreeably surprised to find good pastures and much good land, and a water
ditch, which till April was better than that of Cota, and which
farther on turns out to be suitable for irrigation. I do not
know how to tell Your Reverence the excess of the joy which

filled me on beholding what I scarcely believed, and the facility with which some water could be taken out, in a natural way, and promised me greater abundance. I went there in the beginning of February with fifty pickaxes, crowbars, etc., and in four days of brisk activity I had the water running. This year from 900 to 1,000 fanégas of corn were harvested; and for the year which has commenced 92 fanégas of wheat have been sown, which is already sprouting and irrigated, and ten fanégas of barley. I have renovated the old building, and I roofed it with the tiles of the house in which Your Reverence passed the night. It was also whitewashed, and it is in condition that the Governor, Your Reverence, and the rest of the gentlemen and Fathers may come to honor it whenever they please.

"I cannot deny that if many ranchos are prejudicial to the Missions, that of Reyes gave life to this one. Since I accepted the management, mares for breeding, horses for work, cattle to be slaughtered (here all cattle were scarce), hides to be tanned, were the advantages which I began to secure. With what means? With donations for holy Masses, aided by some young cowboys, with persuasions. For instance, we purchased more than 1,000 head of cattle, and lastly when I least thought of it, the Mission gained cattle, mares, horses, and lands with two thousand *pesos* in cash, and again as much in various manufactures of the Mission, with the pleasure of the whole house of Reyes, the applause of the governors, and the amazement of the spectators. Blessed be God for all! With these advantageous measures, I note that against sandbanks of Oso Flaco on the part of Thomas de la Larga, I discovered, on September 10th of this year, a water ditch larger than any I have seen in the province, but with the defect that it soon empties in the estero. However, if the Mission did not have facilities closer by, and less expensive, it would not be difficult for me to profit by it. Nevertheless, I say no more about it, because perhaps it is not expedient. I therefore say that with such advantageous measures, and the care and vigilance, the Mission now has 10,000 sheep and as many cattle, that is to say, much wool for clothing, much meat to eat in the *pozole* and rations, much tallow for sale, and money to obtain invoices and so forth. We count on $5,000 for goods from Mexico this year, and some for securing statues of saints, etc., which if they come as requested will surely please Your Reverence.

"In view of what was already stated, I have abandoned the renglones (rules) of trade, which robbed the Fathers of time, and perhaps harmed the Indians' health, especially the hide and others which always kept the poor things (Indians) perspiring (humedades). Here they lost already in my time more than $10,000; they may therefore, go to the other part to be useful in minding well the fat cattle, and when the government, in time, comes to kill the animals, the fat-bellied stock will place us in an admirable light.

"As God gives us everything, besides the customary help of clothing for all and dresses for the women, annually come from Mexico woolen cloths, handkerchiefs, blue cloth for jackets and pants, shirts, and drawers of cotton cloths, etc., so that every year we dress from 30 to 40 from head to foot, and renew the clothing for others. Thus it is that I observe in the Indians with such efforts much cheerfulness, and that they are willing like a lynx to do whatever is commanded them.

"However, I observe that the Father Presidente will say: According to this the Fathers will be lacking only the wine and brandy of their own growth, for I know that they have rooted out the vineyards. It is true, that in Lalsacupi they have torn up the vineyard; but they have transplanted it to the site near to the place which I call San Francisco, where it bears well according to the samples, one of these may be which the gardener yesterday brought, two kinds of very small grapes. However, while the vineyards are being planted and until they bear, we have made a life-contract with the Ortegas to divide the vineyard in return for the labor of caring and cultivating it. To them goes the account, to us the wine and brandy (of which we require little), from one and the other we have old and new in abundance, made here after the Mayorcan method in new wine presses. Hence, if God grants us life, some day Your Reverence will drink it without pellicle, without sediments, and without bad taste, pure, and clear.

"This is, dear Fr. Presidente, the true state of this Mission; and inasmuch as, thanks to Heaven, there is in addition peace in the house, the labors are somewhat lighter than in other circumstances. Your Reverence will say that I am slow, since it is so long ago that I wrote; but no, I have much to do. However, I have gone to work carefully putting together all that has passed in order to relate to you in one letter what was material for many. From the first day of this month at night it began to rain, and it has been coming down generously until yesterday the 8th of January, and actually it is raining to-day, the 9th, although it is only in small drops. The whole plain is sown with wheat, and being submerged in water, it is a sign to me of a plentiful harvest.

"The scarcity of water, which is experienced here especially, has at times made planting away from the Mission necessary, and consequently requires people for its needs. As that (said rancho)is five leagues distant from here, it is burdensome to come here on Saturday and return Sunday evening on foot, men, women, youths, and old people. In order to avoid that inconvenience, I have thought of a chapel; but we have not decided, because it might be done to-day and tomorrow abandoned. Now we have the scruple because the Indians do not come, and later it would be because the Fathers being unable do not go. I have spoken about a portable altar in order that the Father casually celebrate or when many people assemble there; but what authors explain on the subject, and Popes Clement XI and Benedict XIV determine has dissuaded us. Finally we have resolved to change the people there every fifteen days, and on the one Sunday they assemble there for the Rosary and devotions. We expect your opinion on the matter.

"The understanding of man is supremely limited. This I experience with mine. The more I do not to be ignorant of what I should know, the less am I free of doubts, withal. For the satisfaction, then, which I owe to Your Reverence, and because after all you are my Prelate, I venture to suplicate you to solve the following doubts, which are such to me, indeed."

Father Payéras then propounds ten doubts regarding the observance of various ecclesiastical regulations and of the rules of St. Francis under the peculiar circumstances prevailing in California, and concludes his most valuable statements as follows:

"Inasmuch as the solution of these ten points is so interesting for the interior tranquillity of the missionary, no less than for his daily conduct, he hopes from the goodness of Your Reverence that you will communicate to him some of your copious lights about them. The least of your subjects, and most affectionate Brother, Q. B. S. M.—

Fr. Mariano Payéras.—Purisima Concepcion, January 13, 1810."

In the hand of Fr. Tápis was written below: *"Received on January 26th, at night."*—Fr. Tápis was at that time visiting Mission San Luis Rey.[1]

---

[1] *Santa Barbara Mission Archives.* See for a synopsis of the letter Bancroft, *California*, vol. ii, pp. 123-124.

CHAPTER IV.

Mission Purisima Concepcion at this period thrived remarkably well. From the Account Book of the missionaries we take the following items which demonstrate that the temporal affairs of the Mission were well regulated. Various officials were engaged to serve as mayordomos and mechanics. Thus Francisco Xavier Aguilar commenced to serve, in what capacity is not specified, on March 10, 1811, at $25 and board a month. He seems to have held his position but a short while.

On April 29, 1811, Fr. Payéras hired the carpenter and mason Josef Antonio Ramirez to "assist in making stone troughs, vats, washtubs and drinking fonts. Furthermore, he is to manage a carpentershop. The Mission will pay $200 in silver and board him a year, besides two pounds of chocolate a month." Ramirez, too, seems to have resigned before the lapse of the year, since his name no longer figures in the Accounts.

Whilst paisano laborers received good wages from the Mission, it was different with the Indians of the Mission who labored for white people. Their wages would be 1½ reáles a day or 18 and ¾ cents and board. This went to the Mission fund, of course, as the neophytes needed no money, they being supplied with everything by the Mission. Thus Antonio Reyes, a ranchero, July 27, 1807, had two neophytes begin to work for him. They labored one week for which he owed $2 and 25 cts. Again he owed 9 reáles for one Indian for 6 days. Again 27 reáles for 3 Indians for 6 days. Carpenter Indians appear to have stood higher; for Reyes paid 3 dollars for 12 days work at a carpenter job. Such wages were not paid in cash, but with goods from the Mission Store.

All the laborers and settlers would apply to the Mission for groceries, drygoods, and agricultural products. Antonio Reyes thus owed the Mission on May 22, 1807, $63.25. This amount he was to pay with young horses or colts at $2 each. There was little cash in the country. The missionaries received no cash for their allowance of $400 a year each, nor for the produce which they sold to Mexico. All was exchanged for groceries, drygoods, shoes, church goods, candles, soap, implements, tools and furniture. Invalido Luis Peña secured candles to the value of one reál, then a Rebozo y Coleta for 13 pesos, probably for his wife or daughter.

Wheat at the time was sold for $2.50 a fanéga or hundred weight. Lime at one reál, or 12½ cents, a peck.

The Account Book would repay a thorough study. It would surprise the reader in many ways, not the least surprising would be the number of settlers and military men who figure in the royal octavo volume bound in leather. Nearly one hundred names appear as customers. Among them such prominent people as Lieutenant Raimundo Carrillo, beginning March 30, 1806. Francisco Ortega, Juan Ortega, Ensign Joaquin Maitorena, J. B. Alvarado, Antonio Reyes, etc.

Needless to say, the missionaries in no way profited from the extra income of the store maintained for the white people. They were but stewards. Everything gained went into the Mission Fund for the Indians.

Thus Mission Concepcion prospered in the spiritual as well as the temporal order until near the end of 1812, when a terrible calamity destroyed the buildings beyond repair. In their Annual Report of December 31, 1812, the missionaries in charge, Fathers Payéras and Ripoll, relate what happened as follows:

"The extraordinary and horrible earthquake, which this Mission suffered on the memorable day of the glorious Apostle St. Thomas, entirely destroyed the church and vestry, buried under the walls the various images and paintings, and ruined the greater part of the furniture. The vestments have not suffered because they were inside the cases. Some of the work shops went down, but some more strongly built, may serve as habitations if not for minor uses which require no such security. One hundred houses of neophyte Indians and the *pozolera* or community kitchen, the walls of which were an adobe and a half thick, and roofed with tiles, have become inserviceable. The garden walls of adobe, covered with tiles, have either collapsed or threaten to fall. The damaged portion will scarcely afford material for rebuilding. The furniture and other contents of the Mission have likewise suffered; some of the contents are entirely crushed, some are broken and all are damaged.

"The inclemency of the weather, and the very heavy rainfalls that followed, prevent digging out anything or covering what lies exposed. For the present, we have nevertheless dug out the most valuable things, and we have secured what is urgently needed. We have put up a church of palisades and in the most primitive way we have built two huts which are to serve as habitations for the two Fathers. We shall also go to work constructing from poles and grass what is indispensable until the earth becomes quiet. Experience may teach us the best method for constructing other buildings.[1]

The Fathers appear to have come to the conclusion very soon that it would be better to transfer the Indian community to another locality, and to rebuild the Mission entirely elsewhere than to try to restore the buildings on the old site. They accordingly determined to petition both the Fr. Presidente and the governor to consent to a transfer. The reasons therefore they presented in a letter to each on March 11, 1813, about two months after the disaster. We reproduce the one addressed to Governor Arrillaga, which reads as follows:

"After the Mission of Purisima, on the day of Apostle St. Thomas, last past, had suffered the most violent earthquake, we at once perceived that its buildings, those of the village included, and the walls of the garden, all constructed of adobe, and covered with tiles, were inserviceable. Fearful of the

---

[1] *Informe Anual*, Dec. 31, 1812; *Cal. Arch., St. Pap., Missions* vol. iv, pp. 208-210.

strange disaster which was aggravated by violent floods, we only thought of saving our persons, those of the guards and neophytes in some poor huts, constructing a *jacal* where to celebrate holy Mass, digging out what was most sacred in the destroyed temple, and as much as possible covering the grain for food and planting. When the first shocks had ceased, we observed with wonder that, if God, like a Father, chastizes and afflicts with one hand, with the other He helps and supports: in plain terms, that, if this Mission, as is known, was the one which suffered most, the said chastisement maybe really called the most fortunate on account of sixty gentiles recently baptized, the remarkable and abundant amount of grain planted, and the copious waters which have filled the river and springs prodigiously.

"In view of what this promises we have examined the interior of the granaries, and we have observed with sorrow that all these structures are ruined from the foundations to the roof: that the church is demolished from the foundation up: and that neither Fathers, nor soldiers, nor neophytes will or can, without terror or risk, live in their habitations, which have partly fallen, are partly out of plumb, and all in many parts seriously cracked.

"Los Berros is on the other side (of the river) at the mouth of the cañon of its name opening on the grand plain of Purisima, and on the very pass and *Camino Reál* from Santa Inés to San Luis Obispo. It is the highway which is used by all the herds and horses of the officials on their journeys, which all travel without touching Purisima, save those who have business to transact with its inhabitants, or for having gone astray, or on account of the river which they sometimes cannot pass. From Los Berros to Alsacupi are five quarter leagues, and from here thither the same, which is 2½ leagues, etc.

"Fr. Mariano (Payéras), on account of the infirmities of his companion Father, passed three winters alone while the river was impassable for the missionaries. Either because he wanted to or because it was necessary, one of the two Fathers set out for another Mission. It began to rain and the river

RUINS OF MISSION PURISIMA AT LOMPOC. ETCHING BY HENRY CHAPMAN FORD.

was swollen. He wanted to cross it, but could not. In the meantime his companion fell sick, and being a human being, he died.[2] Here we have a case that may happen every year, on this side of the river." Therefore the Fathers petitioned for the permit to transfer it to the other side.[3]

To Fr. Presidente José Señan the Fathers in their letter of the same date broached additional motives for the transfer, which Fr. Señan under date of March 16, 1813, communicated to the governor. The Fathers informed Fr. Señan that the locality called Los Berros was more level, and therefore less liable to such violent earthquakes. At Los Berros the requisites for a Mission were at hand: firewood, timber, stone, and other material. The land capable of cultivation there was more abundant, and water for irrigation more accessible and bountiful.

Accordingly Fr. Señan informed the governor that he had no objection, but wanted him to approve of the plan.

Governor Arrillaga, thereupon, granted the permission in a letter dated March 30, 1813.[5]

The annual report compiled nine months later, December 31, 1813, contains so much interesting information that it deserves to be reproduced. "To the church" (at Los Berros, the new site), the Fathers write, "we have brought from the destroyed edifice what could be saved and repaired, and what through the mercy of God had remained uninjured by the earthquake. To this were added a chasuble of red satin with galloons of gold enamel, and a black satin cope with wide golden galloons. In the field and in the house are the implements and the tools which have been saved from the horrible earthquake.

"*Nota.* This Mission of Purisima, founded in the plain south of the Rio Santa Rosa, or San Bernardo according to

---

[2] Fr. Ripoll, who wrote the petition, must have meant a secular companion, for no missionary died at Purisima Concepcion until ten years later.

[3] *Archbishop's Archives*, No. 396.

[4] *Archbishop's Archives*, No. 395.

[5] *California Archives, Provincial Records*, vol. xi, p. 276.

the map of Lopez, on the spot called Alsacupi by the natives, and which was destroyed by the dreadful earthquake suffered from December 21st to the last days of the year 1812, by the requisite permits was on April 23, 1813, moved to the dale called Los Berros by the Spaniards, but Amuu by these natives. The site of the new Mission lies five quarter leagues northward of the old Mission, at the end of the said cañada, in the plain north of said river, on the *Camino Real* from Santa Inés to San Luis Obispo. It is 2,300 varas wide from west to east. While the old place lay away from the public highway, the new site is one league nearer to Santa Inés, and one and one-fourth leagues nearer to San Luis Obispo.

"For the time being we have erected such structures as a Mission requires, although on an humble scale as may be imagined, all of palisades and with thatched roofs. Furthermore a church was constructed of poles veneered with adobes. This holds all the people. A garden was also planted with as many trees as were obtainable, and for its irrigation the water from various springs have been collected, which, after running into their tanks or reservoirs, promise to irrigate in abundance.

"In order to maintain the Mission with water independently of that from the river (for this runs short in summer), we are building a small fountain from which a ditch conducts the water to the foot of the Mission for a distance of 400 paces. To secure a greater volume of water, and to irrigate the field in summer, we have continued to this side of the river the same aqueduct that ran from the river to the old Mission. It crosses the river at the old pass of Santa Inés. After fructifying this whole precious district, in due time it will bring to us its crystal and delicious waters to within 500 paces of our doors."[6]

Before describing the work of the Fathers at the new site, let us see what they had accomplished at the original place, now within the limits of the city of Lompoc, which ought to

---

[6] *Informe Anual Santa Barbara Archives*; *Cal. Arch., St. Pap., Missions*, pp. 264-265.

regard it as a hallowed spot, worthy of much more veneration than the heap of adobe on the north side of the Rio Santa Inés. Only ten days after the earthquake, on December 31, 1812, Fathers Payéras and Ripoll sent their usual Annual Report to the Fr. Presidente, from this we learn that during 1812 as many as thirty-three Indian adults (i. e. all over nine years of age), and thirty-one Indian children, besides one white child, were baptized. This brought the number of Baptisms conferred at the old site from the founding of the Mission, hence during the twenty-five years of its existence, to 2,597.

During the same year 1812, thirty-six Indian couples were married. This increased the number of marriages at the old site from the founding to 725.

Likewise during the same year 1812, thirty-two Indian adults, and nine Indian children died. The whole number from the founding being then 1,440. At the time of the report or rather just before the disaster, the Mission harbored, fed, clothed, and educated 489 male and 510 female Indians, or in all 999 neophytes.

The herds at the same time consisted of 4,000 cattle, 12,000 sheep, 60 pigs, 116 mules, and 1,150 horses of every description.

The year 1812 had not been a prosperous one for agricultural products except wheat. In all only 3,000 fanégas of wheat, 50 fanégas of corn, and 27 fanégas of beans could be harvested.[7]

Furthermore it is to be noted that the Mission reached the largest Indian population in its history on 1804, when 1,520 neophytes dwelt there in peace and happiness under the shadow of the Mission Cross. The previous year, 1803, witnessed the largest number of converts, the number baptized being 450. All over nine years had to be instructed in the necessary rudiments of Religion, which not only required

[7] For details on the various products see table at close of volume.

time but patience. In fact the two Fathers, Calzada and Fernández, were unable to accomplish the task. Fr. José de Miguel of Santa Barbara and Fr. Martinez of San Luis Obispo, therefore, came to their assistance.

Fr. Estévan Tápis, although Presidente of the Missions, took Fr. Boscana's place from August 1811 to August 1812, and then called Fr. Antonio Ripoll to Purisima Concepcion as assistant to Fr. Payéras, just in time to witness the destruction of the Mission property.

CHAPTER V.

A heavy task confronted the two Fathers at the outset;
but they were equal to the situation. Fr. Payéras at forty-
four was in the prime of life, and Fr. Ripoll counted only
twenty-eight summers. Both were unusually capable men,
and in zeal for the spiritual welfare of the Indians they were
not surpassed by any of the friars. Hence the calamity of
December 21, 1812, only served to spur them on to more
energetic efforts for the salvation of their dusky wards.

To begin with, the terrified neophytes had to be gathered
together at the new site. It speaks volumes for the kindly
and paternal management of the missionaries that they seem
to have experienced no difficulties whatever in returning the
neophytes to their care. Like so many confiding children, the
neophytes seem to have reappeared at the bare call of the
Fathers, as they felt that their spiritual and temporal well-
being was secure in the hands of the two priests, and that the
Mission was their real and only home. At all events, there is
no evidence that the aid of the soldiers was required. The
Indians assisted in erecting the necessary buildings, and then
with their happy families occupied their new quarters as
though nothing had happened. In fact, a few more joined the
Mission, so that by the end of the first year at Los Berros the
Fathers could report 1,010 souls living in their charge, whereas
at the old site of Algsacupi twelve months before the number
was 999.

Greater difficulties, which taxed the ingenuity, courage,
and patience of the Fathers to the utmost, presented themselves. Practically, a new Mission had to be established. For
such a purpose the friars formerly could count upon $1,000

worth of goods from the Pious Fund, besides their own stipends of $400, likewise in necessary articles for the use of the missionaries. All this aid was cut off by the Hidalgo Revolt raging in Mexico since September 16, 1810. The Missions now were thrown upon their own resources. The Fathers and their neophytes could have managed their affairs very well, and prosperity even would have been the result, but another serious drawback of the Mexican turmoil affected the California Missions disastrously in the course of time. The soldiers, too, and their officers had to go without their wages and salaries which annually came from Mexico. They now and throughout the Mission period insisted that the Indian Missions should maintain them and their families. This was the unjust burden that eventually impoverished the missionary establishments, and led to their complete ruin. It was this state of things which the missionaries faced at the very beginning of their endeavors in the new surroundings. Nevertheless, they did not lose heart, but went to work and made the most of the circumstances, and for the outcome they trusted to Divine Providence.

While the first year, 1813, was exceedingly busy with regard to building operations, nothing of the kind is mentioned in the reports for 1814. Likewise the replies of the Fathers to the *Interrogatório,* or list of thirty-six questions on the origin, habits, etc., of the Indians, which had been sent to California by the Spanish Government in 1814, are missing. Purisima Concepción Mission is the only one of the twenty-one establishments not figuring in the collection on the subject. Hence many interesting items about the Indians of this district are lost: but as the natives of this region differed little, if at all, from those in the region of Santa Inés, what the Fathers of that Mission therefore related about their Indians will apply to the natives of Lompoc Valley and vicinity.

The year 1815 proved most important in building activities. Besides keeping in repair the temporary structures put up in 1813, an unusually large building was erected. The walls were an adobe and a half or about thirty inches thick. An adobe wall ran through the whole length of the structure, thus dividing it into two rows of rooms. This building which was roofed with tiles, measured 100 varas, or nearly 300 feet in length. The width is not stated. It contained the rooms of the two Fathers, the servants, the chapel, rooms for guests, and the remainder were workshops.

In this same year, too, the temporary church built of palisades and veneered with adobes, was strengthened and plastered.

Ignacio Yguera on October 1, 1814, began to serve at Mission Purisima for $12 a month and rations like other mayordomos. On July 20, 1815, Fr. Payéras made a contract with him on the following terms. "The Mission will give, 1:—One dollar for every day on which he works. 2:—His board as heretofore, with the addition of one small bottle of aguardiente every week. It is to be noted that the liquor will be given him when it is made here; it will not be purchased. 3:—One or two men to help him when he needs them. In return for these wages he obliges himself to apply all his knowledge and energy in the service of the Mission, etc. This contract will continue until the church is finished."

During the same year a signal honor came to Mission Purisima Concepcion through its energetic manager, Fr. Mariano Payéras: for the College of San Fernando de Mexico, which was the motherhouse of the California friars, on July 24, 1815, appointed him Presidente of the California Missions. In consequence of the dispositions of a former Bishop of Sonora, to which diocese the territory belonged, the Fr. Presidente also held the office of vicar-general for the Bishop, and he was therefore the head of the Church in California. Fr. Payéras, however, remained at his beloved Purisima, which accordingly during his term was the ecclesiastical headquarters of the territory. He received the notice of his appointment on November 22, and immediately informed Governor Pablo de Solá.[1]

---

[1] *The Missions*, vol. iii, p. 7.

In 1816 a structure 100 varas long and six varas wide was erected. The walls were one adobe, or about twenty inches, thick, and the roofing consisted of tiles. A corridor or covered porch ran along both sides. This building contained the guard-rooms, rooms for the mayordomos, the carpentershop, and weaving rooms.

Another house of adobe, fifty varas long, was constructed from material of previous buildings, and was intended for the sick. Furthermore, some of the first buildings were remodeled and arranged to house infirm women. Señora Guadalupe Briones, according to the Account Book, was engaged as in-firmarian at a salary of five dollars a month and maintenance. She began to serve on November 20, 1817.

The chapel built in the preceding year, as the Fathers in 1816 also report, was decorated as much as Franciscan poverty permitted and the country supplied. Two altar cloths and two altar covers were secured. It will be observed that this was the private chapel in the long house, not the church which stood apart.

An exceedingly interesting information, not found in the annual report, Fr. Payéras notes in the *Libro de Patentes* of the Mission. He writes: "*Note.*—On January 10, 1816, the road from the door of our Mission Santa Inés was measured, and found to be six leagues, three quarters of a league, and 619 varas long. On February 25, 1816, the road was measured from the door of our reception room to that of Mission San Luis Obispo through La Graciosa. It was discovered to be 18 leagues minus 250 varas long. Through the Rancho of San Antonio it was 19 leagues and 550 varas by way of the garden to Matheo. From San Antonio to this place are three leagues and 3,400 varas."

During the year 1817 the Fathers were completing the foundations for a new church, and at the same time they re-paired the temporary church. Between the house wherein dwelt the white families and the Indian rancheria or neophyte village a fountain was constructed and a corresponding lava-tory. For the use of the infirmary and for minor uses in the same patio another fountain was constructed and intended for the special convenience of the neophytes. The water supplied for both fountains is conducted thither a distance of 800 to 1,000 paces by means of pipes and to basins at suitable distances.

A thoughtful step was taken this year which proved the kindly solicitude of the Fathers for everybody, in this case for the travelers. At the Rancho de Larga the report concludes, nine leagues from here, on one side of the highway, a house was constructed of palisades and covered with tules, sufficiently comfortable for the wanderers. It was free and open to every one that might be overtaken on the road by night. At the Mission every traveller was refreshed and kept until he was ready to continue the journey, in which case he was supplied with a horse and provisions to the next Mission. No charges were made. Such was the custom at all Missions.

The sanctuary was not forgotten, although it was difficult now to procure the requisite goods. It seems the Fathers trusted this fancy work to the girls of the *monjério*, that is to say all girls over eleven and unmarried women who dwelt together in a house set apart for them, and by the people called he *monjério* or nunnery, although there was a vast difference between them and real nuns.

At some Missions, when they had found good tutors, the girls proved apt pupils, so that there was little need to look to Mexico for anything but the material. In this year a fine cope was added to the sacristy wardrobe. It had golden galloons, and was intended to be worn by the priest for the first time on the feast of the Resurrection, or Easter Sunday. Damask curtains, linen altar cloths, three surplices, five cassocks of blue material for the altar boys, and three guilded chandeliers for the presbytery are mentioned among the articles secured. Some things it was possible to obtain from the merchant ships of Lima, Peru.

During the year 1818 the church palisades collapsed. On the same site another church edifice was erected of adobe and

MISSION PURISIMA, AS AUTHOR SAW IT IN 1904.

roofed with tiles, but it was not to be permanent. Two
sacristies and a loft were joined to this building.

The articles procured for the church consisted of two red
frontales (antependia), a portapaz of silver, an image of the
Child Jesus half a vara in height, a rich alb, and an altar covering. The Way of the Cross with framed pictures was also
placed along the interior of the church.

For the year 1819, Fr. Payéras, who had been appointed,
Comisario Prefecto for the Franciscans in California, reports
that under the wretched circumstances prevailing nothing
more could be done than keep the buildings and implements
in repair.

In 1820 two sets of altar cards were all that could be
purchased.

In 1821 Fathers Payéras and Rodriguez report that a
cemetery and a belfry were joined to the church. Both were
entirely new, which would seem to mean that the cemetery
had been elsewhere. No other building operations were reported.

Likewise for 1822 the Fathers confined themselves to keeping in repair the structure that existed. For the church, however, some articles were acquired. Six large framed mirrors,
six glass lanterns, and a wheel with numerous little bells for
use in the sanctuary. Three niches were made in the altar
for as many mirrors. These mirrors, about a yard high, usually
in metal frames, were sent from Mexico, where the people are
very fond of them. For what purposes they came to California, and occupied the walls of the churches, we could never
understand. There is no provision made for them in the
Liturgy of the Church. The custom is justly abolished now.

In 1823 the church was enriched with an alb of the finest
linen, and an amice of the same material, both perhaps the
offering and handiwork of some pious Señora or Señorita.
Furthermore a pair of glass cruets with plate, four additional
mirrors, more than a yard high, a pair of chandeliers and six
oil paintings of various saints, were secured. Finally the
sanctuary was entirely re-carpeted.

The field implements were overhauled, repaired and renewed. Finally, ten new houses for the neophyte village were built and roofed with tiles. These were the last buildings put up during Mission period down to 1832.

The report for 1823 was signed by Fr. Antonio Rodriguez only, as Fr. Mariano Payéras worn out with labor and the care of his Mission and from the visitations of the other nineteen Missions, died at his beloved Mission Purisima Concepción on April 28, 1823, only fifty-four years old. A sketch of his active life will be found near the end of the volume. Fr. Ripoll, who had been his assistant during the troublous period of the earthquake and the rebuilding of the Mission at Los Berros, had been called to Mission Santa Barbara in 1815. Fr. Luis Gil succeeded till 1817. Fr. Francisco Ullibarri arrived in October, 1818, to remain till July 1819. He was alone most of the time, as Fr. Payéras had to visit the other Missions. Fathers Antonio Rodriguez, Vincente Oliva, and José Sanchez served for short periods till November, 1821. Fr. Rodriguez, however, took charge in the beginning of March, 1821, though Fr. Payéras remained at the head, until five months after the death of Fr. Payéras. He was succeeded by Fr. Marcos Antonio de Vitoria.

The adobe church erected in 1818, and intended to be but a temporary edifice, seems to have continued the permanent house of worship; for there is nothing on record to show that another was built. It was variously supplied with church goods, as related. In 1825 its main altar was adorned with two statues, one of St. Bonaventure, the Seraphic Doctor of the Church, and the other St. Anthony, the Wonderworker. The statue of the Immaculate Queen also received a new throne, as Fr. Vitoria writes.

Unfortunately, incessant demands of the military government of California that the Mission must contribute towards the maintenance of the territorial soldiers and their families, together with the decrease of the Indian population, especially of the able-bodied men, had exhausted the resources of Mission Purisima, and rendered improvements impossible. In truth the Mission was slowly dying. Fr. Vitoria in 1827 tried hard to effect something besides gratifying the inconsiderate soldiery at the expense of the poor neophytes. "There have been made," he writes, "two small machines for crushing wheat and other seeds, and there have been woven forty-six bolts of rough cloth." The very last addition was an adornment to the main altar in 1831.

It might be reasonably supposed that afflicted Mission Purisima Concepción which was being rebuilt on the other side of the Rio Santa Inés, would be dispensed from contributing to the support of idle soldiers and of their numerous families; but no exception was made. A double burden, therefore, was laid upon the missionaries and their wards. The first demand is noted in the Account Book in words written by Fr. Payéras, but signed by an officer: "By order of Captain and Governor *interino*, Don José Argüello, Sergeant Don Carlos Carrillo came for $800, which I delivered to him for the habilitacion (quartermaster's office) of the Presidio of Santa Barbara. In witness whereof, on October 2, 1814, he signed— Carlos Antonio Carrillo."

This forced cash contribution, so short a time after the transfer of the Mission, will have been the reason why in that year little or no building operations are reported from distressed Purisima.

Here follow some specimen orders from Monterey for which the Mission received nothing but worthless drafts on Mexico. —"On May 7, 1817, went to the presidio of Monterey 50 fanégas (about 83 bushels) of beans at $3.00 a fanéga; 26 fanégas (about 23 bushels) of corn at $2.00 a fanéga; 34 pairs of shoes at 12 reáles ($1.50) per pair.

"On September 14, I delivered to the corporal for the habilitacion 8 fanégas of beans at 20 reáles ($2.50) a fanéga."

"On August 28, I sent to the habilitacion 44 pairs of shoes at 12 reáles a pair," Fr. Payéras writes.

"On October 27 I sent to the habilitacion 4 fanégas of beans at 20 reáles a fanéga. On the last of December I sent 50 blankets each at 14 reáles, and 50 pairs of shoes at 12 reáles each ($1.50).

Monterey was far away, and the goods had to be taken there by pack mules. With them had to go muleteers. It is very probable that the Mission also furnished the transportation, though it is not said in the Account Book. We now see what amount of supplies was furnished to the presidio of Santa Barbara. As the Mission belonged to that military district, it may be inferred that the Mission of Purisima was called upon more frequently. In Fr. Payéras' hand we find that on January 29,. 1818, he writes:

"I sent to the quartermaster fifty blankets at 11 reáles ($1.37). The soldier Anselmo Romero of San Diego received a blanket and provisions to the amount of $3.25, which are to be charged to Santa Barbara.

"On May 26, I sent to the quartermaster 54 pairs of shoes at 12 reáles.

"On June 27, I sent to the habilitacion 64 sarapes, 25 of which were dyed red, at $4.50 each, and the rest at $4.25 each. I also sent four hides dressed white, which at $20 each are worth $80.

"To the soldier Romero, returning from his exile, for two mules and outfit and cowboy to Mission San Luis Obispo, $3.50.

"On October 5, I delivered $300 in silver to Ensign Maytorena for the habilitacion.

"On December 16, I sent to the habilitacion Maytorena 70 blankets at 11 reáles each.

"On January 14, 1819, I sent 26 blankets at 12 reáles, and six at $3.00—$48.00.

"For what Bruno Avila took out for his recruits—$4.50.

"For two saddles I delivered to Ensign Don Mariano Estrada for the recruits on July 13,—$27.50.

"For shoes and provisions to the old invalid soldier Sotelo, 14 reáles.

"To Ensign Mariano Estrada for six pack mules and outfit besides two cowboys to San Luis Obispo—$8.00.

"To the soldier Castro banished to San Diego for three pack mules and outfit and muleteer to Santa Inés, $4.75; for flour and cheese—9 reáles.

"On the 18th of September, for the presidio of Loreto (Lower California), I delivered to Sergeant José M. Arce, ten weapons at $5.00, and various other articles, to the amount of $91.75, or in all—$146.75.

These accounts in the book before us run to the year 1823, inclusive, when probably another book was opened to record contributions to the military, and deliveries for which never anything was paid but a worthless draft on Mexico. Under these circumstances the Mission could not thrive, and the peace of the Indians was at an end.

CHAPTER VI.

We now approach a sad episode in the history of Mission
Purisima concepción. It is nothing less than a bloody uprising
of the neophytes. The endless exactions of the military, and
the overbearing conduct of the guards, at last aroused the
unusually patient converts of three Missions to turn upon
their tormentors. Revolts would have occurred ere this, and
they would have extended over a wider territory, had not the
kindly missionaries, themselves variously oppressed, by word
and example induced their wards to submit and to hope
and pray for better times. Those better times, however, would
never appear. Although the older neophytes, at least of Santa
Inés, where the trouble started, cautioned against violence,
the younger generation had heard of the rebellion in Mexico
and how it was conducted. They began to chafe under the
everlasting demands for supplies to feed, clothe, and equip the
soldiers and their families, whilst the neophytes themselves
and their families suffered want in consequence.[1] It needed
but a spark to fire the wrath of the Indians. This was furnished
by an inconsiderate petty officer at Santa Inés named Corporal
Cota. He ordered a neophyte to be flogged, and thus brought
on the disorders which under a capable leader might have en-
dangered the peace of the whole territory. It seems that some
of the Indians of Santa Inés conspired with those of Mission
Purisima. At all events, the only one killed at Santa Inés,
where the outbreak occurred on Saturday afternoon, Feb-

---

[1] "Los Indios se quejan amargamente de que estan trabajando para
que coman los soldados, y que nada se les paga de su sudor y su trabajo."
The Missions and Missionaries, vol. iii, p. 195.

ruary 21, 1824, was a Purisima neophyte named Cipriano. He was buried by the Indians on the same day in the cemetery adjoining the Mission church. The guards and Fr. Francisco X. Uria withdrew to the main building, and there defended themselves all through the night and the next morning, when Sergeant Anastasio Carrillo with troops arrived from Santa Barbara, and caused the Indians to abandon the fight. Fr. Uria, who seems to have offended some of the young neophytes, perhaps reproved them severely, retired to Santa Barbara.

Runners brought the news of the battle to Purisima on the same Saturday, February 21, this caused the Indians there to take possession of the Mission. According to Bancroft,[2] Corporal Tibúrcio Tapia with his four or five guards defended themselves and their families in their quarters all through the night, only one woman being wounded, but surrendered on Sunday when the powder had given out. The soldiers and their families were then allowed to withdraw to Santa Inés with Fr. Blas Ordáz, who had been stationed at Purisima since April, 1823. Fr. Antonio Rodríguez, the senior missionary, remained with his excited neophytes, who, as Bancroft points out, showed no disposition to molest him. They had no quarrel with the missionaries; but they deeply despised the selfish and unkind soldiery.

During the excitement of the first night of the revolt, one neophyte, named Estéban, properly belonging to Santa Barbara, and four strangers were killed. These four men had been unaware of any trouble when they approached Purisima on their way to Los Angeles. Details are lacking entirely. The names of the four unfortunate travellers were Dolores Sepulveda, Ramón Sotelo, Simon Colima, and Mansisidor de Loreto. Fr. Blas Ordáz buried the bodies of the five men in the Mission cemetery on February 23, 1824. This shows that Tapia and his following could not have left for Santa Inés until that day, since Fr. Ordáz accompanied them.[3]

---

[2] *California*, vol. ii, pp. 527-529.

[3] *Libro de Entierros de Purisima. The Missions*, vol. iii, p. 196.

The Purisima neophytes now prepared to defend themselves against the soldiers, who they well knew would be sent
from Santa Barbara or Monterey. They erected palisade
fortifications, cut loop-holes in the adobe walls of the church
and of other buildings, and mounted two swivel guns which
had been used to make appropriate noise on feast days. They
also sent messengers to the neophytes and gentiles elsewhere,
but it was nearly a month before any soldiers appeared. The
troops at Santa Barbara had their hands full subduing the
neophytes of that Mission, whereas governor Luis Argüello
seems to have encountered some difficulty in collecting and
equipping a force sufficient for a campaign. However, let us
hear the report of the commanding officer, Lieutenant José
Maria Estrada, who writes to the governor as follows: "I
have the satisfaction of placing before Your Honor for your
further action the happy outcome secured against the factious
neophytes of the said Missions of Santa Inés and Purisima by
the valiant troops whom I have the honor to command and
the account of which is as follows:

"Having left the Mission of San Luis Obispo, the point of
our reunion or let it be called quartel general, where we assembled to the number of 109, enlisted as artillery, infantry, and
cavalry, with a field piece of four pounds. With this force I
began my march to Purisima on the 14th of the present month
of March. At the site of *Oso Flaco* the division passed the night
after the precautions of war had been taken. In this place our
advanced guard surprised two hostile couriers, who came from
San Luis Obispo, which they had already reached on the 12th
with three others. On the 15th, the march continued without
any thing of note, and then we camped at the foot of the Cuesta
de La Graciosa. On the 16th, at two o'clock in the morning,
after we had overcome indescribable obstacles on account of
the declivity of the mountain, we succeeded in ascending and
in dragging the cannon by hand. Observing that it was about
time to operate it, after having placed it under cover for protection along with the munitions in charge of 28 horsemen
under a corporal. I commanded that two advance guards,

each composed of fifteen horsemen under the command of corporals Nicolas Alviso and Trinidad Espinosa, to separate to the right and the left, and in a circular movement proceed toward the Mission in order to prevent the flight of rebels, and make them meet our forces. In this manner, step by step, we approached the Mission until we were within shooting distance of our cannon. Protected by thirty-three infantrymen, this began firing at about 8 a. m., always advancing until we reached within shooting range of our muskets. From their loopholes the Indians poured out a lively gun-fire at us with their one pound cannon, and also sent out a shower of arrows. Boldly despising that resistance, the artillery replied with brilliantly directed shots, and the musketry with a not less active firing.

"It seemed that the Indians wanted to take to flight, but seeing that the cavalry had completely surrounded them, and that Don Francisco Pacheco with twenty horsemen and drawn sword hastened to intercept them, the Indians could not help seeing that they were completely cut off. They then availed themselves of the advocacy and favor of Fr. Antonio Rodríguez the missionary of said Mission. He agreed to their clamors, and sent a written supplication that the firing cease, and then he appeared openly in person. I commanded that firing stop. It was half past ten in the morning. The casualties of this glorious battle won by the small number of eighty men against 400 Indians equipped with all weapons[4] were three wounded, one, the late militia-man Dionisio Rios, was mortally wounded, the other two only slightly so. On the side of the rebels sixteen were killed and a considerable number wounded. Their two pedreros (swivel guns) were taken, besides sixteen muskets, 150 lances, six machetes (cutlasses), and an incalculable number of bows and arrows.—Quartel General of Purisima, March 19, 1824. José Maria Estrada."[5]

[4] Fortunately for the soldiers the Indians were not well equipped to fight a party armed with firearms, as Estrada himself shows in enumerating the booty. With the muskets and the toy cannon they knew how to make a noise, but not how to hit the mark.

[5] *California Archives, Dept. State Papers*, vol. i, pp. 574-576.

Captain de la Guerra, with troops from Santa Barbara, arrived after the rebels had surrendered, as Bancroft relates. Under orders from the governor, he and Estrada took the depositions of the prisoners, and on March 23 decreed the punishment. Seven of the Indians were condemned to death for complicity in the murder of Sepulveda and his three companions. The sentence was executed at Purisima on March 26. Fr. Antonio Rodríguez in the Burial Register enters the names, etc., as follows: *"Pasados por las Armas.* On the 26th day of March, 1824, in the cemetery of the church of this Mission of Purisima, I gave ecclesiastical burial to the bodies of the following neophytes:"

José Andrés, husband of Clara, 37 years old;
Felipe, husband of Maria Rosário, 30 years old;
Etines, single, 29 years of age;
Antonio, husband of Anatólia, 25 years old;
Estévan, single, 22 years of age;
Pacifico, widower, 27 years old;
Baltasar, husband of Flora, 30 years of age.

"All these seven neophytes received the Sacraments of Penance and Holy Eucharist, and disposed themselves with religious piety. In witness whereof I have signed this.—Fr. Antonio Rodríguez."[6]

The four ringleaders of the revolt, Mariano, Pacomio, Benito, and Bernabe, according to Bancroft, were sentenced to ten years in the presidio and perpetual exile from the province. Eight others were punished with eight years of imprisonment at the presidio.[7]

It will be observed that of the seven men executed only one was over thirty years of age. This shows, what tradition of the Indians at Santa Inés maintains, that the revolt was the work of the young generation. The older men kept aloof. Furthermore the claim of Estrada that his eighty men had to face 400 well equipped Indians, is a mighty exaggeration.

---

[6] *Libro de Entierros, Purisima Mission.*
[7] *California* vol. iii, p. 532.

They were not well equipped according to his own showing, nor could there have been 400 warriors in the affray or Estrada might have fared badly. The Indian population of the Mission at the end of 1823, less than three months previous to the battle, was exactly 722 men, women, and children. Three-fifths, or about 430, could not bear arms, since they included women, children, aged and infirm. That would leave at most about 290 able-bodied Indians. If we eliminate all men over forty years of age, who would have nothing to do with the uprising, we shall have a fighting force of about 150 men, whose weapons consisted of bows and arrows, since the muskets discovered among them in their hands were about as formidable as clubs. The two little cannons did no harm either, except that they frightened the babies by the noise. So the victory was not such a glorious affair as described in Estrada's fulsome report.

It might be supposed that the sad spectacle of seven of their able-bodied men being shot to death as criminals, would have completely discouraged and embittered the neophytes, and caused them to abandon the Mission. Scarcely any one, however, forsook their kindly missionary home. There were drawbacks, and all had to labor for the soldiers of California without any compensation, and without receiving recognition even; but it was not the fault of the missionary, who suffered the same privations and ingratitude. So older heads counseled that all remain where most of them had been born and reared under the paternal care of the good Father. Hence it is that on December 31, 1824, the Mission population had decreased by only sixty souls. Eight of these had been killed, twelve had been imprisoned and exiled. This left forty to be accounted for, or fifty-eight, with eighteen additions in the Baptismal Register. During the year, not counting the eight victims of the revolt, 77 had died, however. This explains that the decrease in population was about the same as in previous years, as the death-rate in comparison to the Baptisms was four to one.

Why the mortality was so great has been explained in our

larger work *The Missions and Missionaries*, vol. ii, pp. 500, 501, 519, 608-609, 620; and vol. iii, pp. 29-30, 79. In consequence of this, all the Indians of the district having been converted, the Mission population dwindled steadily from year to year, as the reader will learn from consulting the Tables at the end of this volume. At the close of 1832, when the missionary made his last annual report, the neophyte population consisted of 227 male and 145 female Indians—372 in all. By that time the Mission of Purisima Concepción, since its founding in 1787, had baptized 3,256, nearly all Indians, blessed the marriages of 1,020 Indian couples, and buried, 2,633 dead.

On the same date Fr. Vitoria reported 9,000 cattle, 3,500 sheep, 20 goats, 65 pigs, 1,000 horses, and 200 mules, still belonging to the Mission community.

In the same year, 1832, 71 fanégas (118 bushels) of grain had been planted, but yielded only 699 fanégas (1,165 bushels).

CHAPTER VII.

The young Californians of Mexican extraction, instead of
curbing their desires in keeping with the Seventh and Tenth
Commandments of God, which they had learnt, in their child-
hood, on the arrival in 1825 of José M. Echeandia, first Mexican governor after the Independence of Mexico, hearkened to
the doctrines and notions of irreligious foreigners. The consequence was that they, too, like their unscrupulous mentors,
coveted the lands cultivated by the neophytes, and the herds
reared by the Mission Indians. There was plenty of land
which they might have preempted and tilled, but that is just
what their indolence would not agree to. So they concocted
a scheme to secure possession of the lands, the livestock, and
even of the Indians, who should continue to labor for them.
Governor José Figueroa in 1834 was intimidated into issuing
a so-called secularization decree without even waiting for the
approval or consent of the Mexican Government. The reader
will find the details in our Volume Three of the General
History.

The final legislation confiscating the Missions, was not
published till November 4, 1834. With regard to Purisima
Mission, the hungry office seekers appear to have been in a
hurry. At all events, a commissioner to take over the estate
was appointed in the person of Domingo Carrillo, as early as
the 30th of the same month. The property was appraised on
February 18, 1835, by William G. Dana and Santiago Lugo.
The inventory was signed and the temporalities formally

delivered to the commissioner by Fr. Marcos Vitoria on March 1, 1835. José Antonio Dominguez was named mayordomo.[1]

The property was valued as follows:

Main building with 21 rooms	$ 4,300.00
Twelve minor structures	1,205.00
Furniture in the main building	2,001.00
Goods in the warehouse	6,255.75
Grain and other produce	4,821.50
Vestments and other valuables in the church	4,944.12
Library with 139 volumes	655.75
Five bells	1,000.00
Three gardens	728.50
Cattle (at the Mission)	201.75
Church structure	400.00
Site of the Mision Viega at Lompoc, first Mission site	373.50
Site at Jalama	784.50
Rancho Los Alamos	1,185.00
" San Antonio	1,418.00
" Santa Lucia	1,080.00
" San Pablo	1,060.00
" Todos Santos	7,176.00
" Guadalupe	4,065.00
" La Mision	1,952.00
Livestock at large	16,369 00
Total Valuation	$61,976.37
Debts	1,218.50
	60,757.87

The original document gives a total valuation of $62,585.00, including credits, or dues from individuals, to the amount of $3,613.00, which does not correspond with the valuation as itemized.[2]

On August 18, 1835, Domingo Carrillo turned the Mission over by inventory to his brother Joaquin Carrillo. In this inventory the goods in the warehouse, grain, iron implements, the tools in the bakery, smithy, carpentershop, shoeshop,

[1] *California Archives, State Papers, Missions,* vol vi, pp. 437-487; *State Papers Missions,* vol. xi, pp. 280-287.
[2] *California Archives, State Papers, Missions* vol. vi, pp. 437-487.

weaving rooms, mill, etc., are valued at $29,981. The credits amounted to $1,774.00; the debts to $1,371.62.[3]

A memorandum signed by Fr. Juan Moreno gives the following statistics to date, December 31, 1834:

Baptisms (since the founding)						3,314
Marriages						1,040
Deaths						2,687
Indians on the Mission roll						407
Confessions, Easter, in 1834						37
Communions, Easter, in 1834						37
Viaticum administered						7
Communions, Easter, of whites						2
Cattle						6,200
Sheep						6,458
Pigs						40
Goats						16
Mules						70
Horses						1,200
Wheat harvested in 1834		613	fanégas or		1,020	bushels
Barley	"	"	302	" "	503	"
Corn	"	"	150	" "	250	"
Beans	"	"	115	" "	192	"
Peas	"	"	30	" "	50	"
Horse beans	"	"	8	" "	13	"
Lentils	"	"	8	" "	13	"
Garbanzos	"	"	2	" "	3	"

If we may believe Bancroft, who forgot to indicate his authority, "the building of a new church was contemplated this year in (1835), the old one being in a sad state; but nothing was apparently accomplished."[4] The item is important in that it shows that divine service was celebrated in a separate church building, outside the long building, as late as 1835, at least. A room was arranged in the west end of the long building for a chapel when the church became inserviceable.

From Bancroft we learn that on June 15, 1838, Carrillo by inventory delivered the management of the Mission tempor-

---

[3] *California Archives, State Papers, Missions,* vol. vi, p. 16. Bancroft Collection. Compare Bancroft, vol. iii, p. 665.

[4] Bancroft, vol iii, p. 665.

alities to José Maria Valenzuela, the amount noted being
$27,394. In 1839, Emigdio Salgado is mentioned as mayor-
domo under Valenzuela, and Juan Salgado *Ilavero*, or keeper
of the keys. The salaries of the administrators, mayordomo
de campo, and *Ilavero* amounted to $982, very probably for
the quarter of the year. There is no mention of a missionary,
because from about 1836 the Franciscans attended it from
Santa Inés. In February 1839, more than 600 sheep drowned
in the floods. The Indian population at the time, February
28, was 242 souls.[5]

In January, 1839, William E. P. Hartnell, a convert
Englishman, was appointed inspector of the Missions. An
inventory drawn up on July 25, 1839, gives the Indian population at the Mission as 122, many of them being sick, besides
47 freed neophytes at Los Alamos. He found that the property
still consisted of 3,824 cattle, 1,300 sheep, 1,532 (?) horses,
90 mules, 3½ barrels of wine, 3½ barrels of brandy, 1,500
lbs. of tallow, 550 lbs. of lard, 100 hides, 99 tanned skins, 210
fanégas of grain, etc. Sixty fanégas, or 100 bushels, of wheat
and barley had been planted, and the crops looked well. The
debts, however, amounted to $3,696. The surviving neo-
phytes were content with their administrator Valenzuela, but
wished the return of their missionary, Fr. Moreno preferably.
At the request of the Indians, Hartnell removed the keeper
of the keys, Juan Salgado. Hartnell also permitted the
slaughter of 300 cattle to purchase $800 worth of clothing for
the neophytes. The 47 Indians at Los Alamos were anxious
to keep their lands, and José A. de la Guerra, the grantee,
promised in writing not to molest them.[6]

Fr. José Joaquin Jimeno of Mission Santa Inés, on October
17, 1840, in virtue of governor Alvarado's Reglamento, Article
29, proposed Eugenio Ortega as mayordomo, who accordingly
was appointed to succeed Valenzuela, by Bancroft mentioned

    [5] Bancroft, vol. iii, pp. 665-666.
    [6] *Archbishop's Archives* number 2252. *Missions and Missionaries*, vol.
iv, p. 168.

as mayordomo also at Santa Barbara Mission in 1838-1839.[7]

Perhaps Valenzuela returned or never surrendered the office, for on July 1, 1841, he writes to José Antonio de la Guerra that, after the inventory had been drawn up, he delivered to him the vestments, sacred vessels, and other treasures of the church of said pueblo of Purisima.[8] It would seem from this that the old church was abandoned at this time, if not before, and a room in the long house arranged for divine services.

The French traveller Duflot de Mofras visited Mission Purisima some time in 1841 or early in 1842. He found that "Mission Purisima Concepción is situated seventeen leagues west-north-west from Mission Santa Inés, between Point Concepción and Point Argüello, four miles from the sea, on the bank of a river. At present, it is almost entirely ruined. There is no missionary there, and only some sixty Indians are seen. As to the livestock, this amounts barely to 800 head of cattle, 3,500 sheep, and 300 horses. Yet in 1834 the Mission counted 900 neophytes, 15,000 head of horned livestock, 2,000 horses, 14,000 sheep, and harvested 6,000 fanégas of cereals." Where Mofras picked up these figures is a mystery. At the end of 1834 the Mission counted no more than 407 neophytes, 6,200 cattle, 6,458 sheep, and 1,200 horses of all kinds and ages. Furthermore, only 1,228 fanégas of cereals were harvested. In its best years the Mission never reached the figures offered by Mofras. Colton, a sectarian preacher, who came with the Americans in 1846, and then held the office of alcalde at Monterey, surpassed Mofras. According to Colton, Mission Purisima in 1830 owned 40,000 cattle, 30,000 sheep, 2,600 tame horses, 4,000 mares, and 5,000 pigs! Whereas in 1830, as the reader will find in the Table later on, the Mission possessed 7,000 cattle, 6,000 sheep, 1,000 horses, and 50 pigs. Had the Fathers reported contrary to the truth, the Cali-

[7] *California*, vol. iii, p. 657.
[8] *California Archives, State Papers, Missions*, vol. xi, pp. 288-303.

fornians under the Picos, Alvarados, Vallejos, etc., would have howled, and the governor would have investigated.[9]

Colton also claims, with equal truth, that so many cattle remained even after the priest in charge, whom he fails to name, had instituted a free-for-all slaughter. "Its lands (Mission) covered about 1,300 (?) square miles, and were at one time so filled with wild cattle, that the presiding priest granted permits to any person who desired to kill them for their hides and tallow, the meat being thrown away. Thousands in this shape fell under the lasso and the knife."

It would seem that Hittéll, Guin, etc., took their clue for their preposterous figures on the wealth of the missions from this same Colton. The official reports, as shown by the Tables, will convince the reader that all such descriptions are pure fiction.

According to Bancroft, José Antonio de la Guerra was administrator in 1841-1842, that is to say from July 1, 1841. He was accused of having dissipated what was left of the Mission property of any value. Ere three months had elapsed he was ordered to deliver the property to Miguel Cordero of Santa Inés, but refused unless he were paid $700 for which he claimed to be personally responsible to creditors of the Mission. In February, 1842, de la Guerra (who must not be confounded with the noble José de la Guerra of Santa Barbara) at length made the delivery to Cordero as required. The latter, however, found that the property, except some inserviceable furniture, had disappeared, and that José Antonio de la Guerra had killed and scattered the livestock on pretext of orders from the (Alvarado's) government. Fr. José J. Jimeno also accused Antonio de la Guerra of having robbed the Mission of everything, for which charge he said he had irrefutable proofs. Notwithstanding that the Mission was in a dying condition, the demands from the military continued, and the surviving neophytes had to labor to meet the orders for supplies. In April, 1842, for instance, the mayordomo,

---

[9] Mofras, *Exploration*, vol. i, pp. 275-276; Colton, *Three years in California*, p. 448.

Diego Fernández, was informed that the yearly contribution of the Mission to the presidio was 20 fanégas of corn, 10 fanégas of beans, 1,000 lbs. of tallow, 70 pairs of shoes, and $25 worth of soap.[10]

Such endless demands, together with the salaries of the superfluous officials, made it impossible for the Mission to recover. It was doomed to extinction in a short time, as everything rapidly went to ruin. All the other Missions were in a similar predicament from the same causes. The new governor, Manuel Micheltorena, observed as much soon after his arrival from Mexico in August, 1842. In obedience to instructions from the General Government of Mexico, he therefore issued his memorable decree of March 29, 1843, which restored the management of the Mission temporalities, or what was left of them, to the Franciscan Fathers. We have no details of the transfer of Mission Purisima Concepción, except that the administrator Miguel Cordero delivered the remnants of the once most flourishing establishment, and that Fr. Juan Moreno complying with the advice of Commissary Prefect Fr. Narciso Durán, accepted the charge, but continued to reside at Mission Santa Inés.

It is a pity that the poor Father omitted to describe the situation for the benefit of posterity. What a difference would there be between his report and that of Fr. Payéras less than thirty years previously! What he must have felt may be inferred from a laconical report made by Fr. Duran at the special request of the Mexican Government on February 29, 1844, about ten months after the restoration of the Missions to the Fathers. Writing of Mission Purisima the Fr. Commissary says: "After nine years of secularization there remain neither property nor lands to cultivate. It may still count on a moderate vineyard. It is in charge of the Rev. Fr. Juan Moreno, who is very ill, but who has an assistant in the person of the recently ordained priest, Rev. Miguel Gomez. The

---

[10] Bancroft, vol. iv, pp. 647-648.

population may be about two hundred souls."[11] A glorious
result of the iniquitous transaction called "secularization!"

Worse was still to come. Micheltorena, for his endeavors
to resurrect the Missions by taking them out of the hands of
the gang headed by Pio Pico and Alvarado, was compelled to
leave the country in January, 1845. Pico himself then reached
the goal of his ambition. He assumed the office of governor
of California, and without waiting for the approval of the
General Government of Mexico, nay in spite of it, proceeded
to wipe out the Missions with the aid of a subservient assembly
of fewer than half a dozen henchmen. Afraid lest the Mission
property should escape their greed, they first forbade the
missionaries to sell or give away anything, although the same
Fathers had created the wealth of the Missions, and appropriated nothing to themselves or to their own Mother College.
Some of the Fathers resented the insult, and so protested.
Fr. Moreno in reply only wrote in April 26, 1845: "On my
own authority I have not done away with anything, or sold
or donated anything worth notice or needful. If the only
piece of ground which remained (and which, if sold with the
previous knowledge of the government, I hoped would cover
the old debt due to Mr. Thompson), was recently given
away, and which might amount to thirty yards of the ranch,
it was not my fault, but that of the (Pico) government, which
gave it away against my will."[12]

More light is thrown on the situation by another letter of
Fr. Moreno to Pico dated June 20, 1845, only two months
later. "Señor," he writes, "I do not wonder having received
no reply to the letters which I wrote to Your Honor, considering the many occupations in which you will be immersed; but
I find it necessary to molest Your Honor again, because Mr.
Thompson was here a few days ago, and pressed me for the
payment of the account he had against Mission Purisima of
which I am the missionary and which is in my care. I had a

[11] *The Missions*, vol. iv, p. 322.
[12] *The Missions*, vol. iv, p. 356.

year ago promised to pay him the whole amount, or the greater portion, in the hope that I should have permission to sell the site called Santa Rita; but now the government (Pio Pico), to my surprise, has arranged to cede it to some one else, who is Ramon Malo, so that I am unable to pay the debt, inasmuch as the Mission had no property whatever. As this was the only piece of land that remained, it is the more painful to me as it was given away without adhering to the requirements of the law which have always been observed, and which are just and necessary. In this a grave wrong has certainly been done to me and to the Mission in my charge—the greatest damage indeed. I therefore herewith protest against this grant in order that I may at any time appeal to another judge so that he may declare this act illegal, and restore the tract to its lawful owner."[13]

Pico was probably under obligations to Malo, and so he just gave him that last piece of Purisima Mission land, neither caring about the needs or the wishes of the poor Indian owners, nor how Thompson might come by what was due him. The discouraged Fr. Moreno soon had occasion to appeal the case to the Highest Judge, for he died just six months later, December 27, 1845, and Pico's misrule was cut short by the raising of the United States flag in the following July.

Pico was not yet satisfied. The Mission buildings and the site remained still to be disposed of ere the Mission could be said to have been wiped out. On May 28, 1845, he had his subservient assembly composed of Narciso Botello, F. X. Figueroa, Carlos Carrillo, Ignacio del Valle, decree the sale of Purisima along with San Rafael, San Francisco or Dolores, Soledad and San Miguel. In obedience to this illegal decree of the assembly, Pico declared, in a proclamation of October 28, 1845, that these Missions would be sold at auction to the highest bidder. The first three Missions to suffer the disgrace of coming under the hammer, a proceeding which would have horrified Fr. Serra as a Sacrilege, were San Juan Capistrano, Purisima Concepción, and San Luis Obispo. On December 4,

1845, Purisima was given to John Temple for $1,110.[14] "The titles were issued on December 6, 1845, although the price was not in all cases paid, nor full possession given, until the next year."[15]

Thus came to an end Mission Purisima Concepción within two days of the 58th anniversary of its founding by Fr. Fermin de Lasuén, the successor of Fr. Junípero Serra.

---

[14] Pio Pico himself wrote, doubtless not a little elated with his triumph over the Missions; "Habiendose puesto en publica subhasta, y el mejor postor de la venta del edificio principal de la *Purisima*, Viñas de Jalama, tierras y muebles de dicha, resultando comprado de lo mencionado, Juan Temple, como mejor postor, en la cantidad de $1,110!—

[15] *California Archives, State Papers, Missions*, vol. xi, pp. 907-909.

See also *The Missions*, vol. iv, pp. 445, 458, 460. The whole transaction of Pio Pico and his subservient legislators regarding the Mission property was declared null and void by the U. S. Land Commission and by the U. S. Court, on the ground that Pico had no authority to sell the lands of the Missions. See *The Missions and Missionaries of California*, volume iv, Part III, Chapters XI and XII. Hence the Patent issued reproduced in the next chapter.

CHAPTER VIII.

THE UNITED STATES OF AMERICA

To All Whom These Presents Shall Come, Greeting:

Whereas, it appears from a duly authenticated transcript filed in the General land office of the United States, that pursuant to the provisions of the Act of Congress approved the third day of March one thousand eight hundred and fifty-one entitled "An Act to ascertain and settle the private Land Claims in the State of California," Joseph Sadoc Alemany, Roman Catholic Bishop of the Diocese of Monterey in the State of California, a corporation sole, filed his petition on the nineteenth day of February Anno Domini one thousand eight hundred and fifty-three with the Commissioners to ascertain and settle the Private Land Claims in the State of California, sitting, as a Board in the City of San Francisco in which petition he claimed the confirmation to himself and his successors of the title to certain Church property in California "to be held by him and them in trust for the religious purposes and uses to which the same have been respectively appropriated," said property consisting of "Churches, edifices, houses for the use of the Clergy and those employed in the service of the Church, Churchyard, burial grounds, gardens, orchards and vineyards, with the necessary buildings thereon, and appurtenances"—the same having been recognized as the property of said Church by the laws of Mexico, in force at the time of the cession of California to the United States: And whereas, the Board of Land Commissioners aforesaid on the eighteenth day of December, Anno Domini, one thousand eight hundred and fifty-five rendered a decree of confirmation in favor of the petitioner for certain lands described therein to be held in the capacity and for the uses set forth in his petition," the land of the Mission de la Purisima being described as follows to wit: "The Church and building occupied as a dwelling adjoining it, constituting the Church Mission buildings of the Mission of la Purisima, situated in Santa Barbara County, together with the land on which the same are erected, and the Courtyard fenced in adjoining the buildings in the rear and the curtilage and appurtenances thereto belonging and also the Cemetery belonging to the said Mission with the limits as established by the adobe wall by which the same is surrounded including however within the limits the land covered by the old Church now in ruins. Also a garden situated about half a mile North East of said buildings known as "the Mission Garden, with the fence by which the same is enclosed for its boundaries, being the same which is delineated on Map numbered in the Atlas before referred to on which it is designated, by the word "orchard," which said decree or decision having been taken by appeal to the District Court of the United States of America for the northern District of California, and the Attorney General of the United States having given notice that appeal in the cause entitled "The United States vs. J. S. Alemany,"—L. C. 609—would not be prosecuted, and a stipulation to that effect having been entered into by the United States Attorney, the said District Court on the Sixteenth day of March in the year of our Lord one thousand eight hundred and fifty-seven, on motion of the United States District Attorney "ordered, adjudged and decreed that claimant have leave to proceed under the decree of the U. S. Land Commissioners heretofore rendered in his favor as under final decree.

And whereas under the 13th section of said Act of 3d March, 1851, and the supplemental legislation and in accordance with the proceedings had pursuant to said Act and supplemental legislation there was deposited in the General Land office of the United States a return with the descriptive notes, certificate of advertisement and plat of the survey of the said claim confirmed as aforesaid, authenticated by the signature of the United States Surveyor General for the State of California which said survey was rejected by decision dated the sixteenth day of June, Anno Domini, one thousand eight hundred and seventy-three of the Commissioner of the General Land Office.

And whereas under the aforesaid 13th Section of said Act of 3d March, 1851, and the supplemental legislation and in accordance with the proceedings had pursuant to said Act and supplemental legislation there has been deposited in the General Land Office of the United States a return with the descriptive notes and plat of the survey of the said Claim confirmed as aforesaid authenticated by the signature of the United States Surveyor General for the State of California and made in accordance with the aforesaid decision of the Commissioner of the General Land Office, which said descriptive notes and plat of survey are in the words and figures following, to wit;

"Tract No. 1.—Orchard—"Commencing at a post No. 1, from which a pear tree ten inches in diameter (being the most westerly tree in the orchard) bears north sixty-four degrees East twenty-four links distant, "Thence the variation of the magnetic needle being fourteen degrees and fifteen minutes East, North thirty-seven degrees and fifteen minutes East, "At seven chains and fifty links center of reservoir fifty-four links in diameter bears South fifty degrees East, two hundred links distant, At eight chains and five links an old aqueduct course South East and ascends—At ten chains and fifty-four links fence near its North corner course South East—and thirteen chains and twenty-one links to post No. 2, in earth mound Station; Thence descending South fifty-two degrees and thirty minutes East—At six chains enters Valley, course East and West—"At nine chains and nineteen links a post marked N. 3 Station a willow tree twelve inches in diameter bears North fifty-one degrees West two chains and forty-two links distant, Thence S. 37 degrees 15′ W, gradually ascending course S. W. At one chain ascend and thirteen chains and twenty-eight links to post No. 4 in earth mound Station, a house built by Ramon Malo stands in a Westerly direction, about three hundred links distant, Thence North fifty-two degrees and fifteen minutes West descending—At sixty-five links fence and enters Valley, course South West, and nine chains and nineteen links to the place of beginning, containing twelve acres and nineteen one hundredths of an acre (12 19/100) and designated upon the plat of public surveys as, Lot numbered thirty-seven Township seven, North Range thirty-four West S. B. M.

"Tract No. 2.—Mission Building and old Ruins, "Beginning at a post marked No. 1 at the East corner of old ruins and— "Thence the variation of the magnetic needle being fourteen degrees and fifteen minutes West "At twenty links East corner of Mission Buildings "At one chain and twelve links, a new fence course S. E. "At two chains and forty-two links new fence course South East "At three chains and forty links East corner Church, 'At four chains and sixty-six links South corner Church and leave Mission Building and nine chains and twenty-five links to post No. 2 in earth mound, Station "Thence North forty-three degrees and forty-five minutes West one chain and twenty-one links to post No. "3" in stone mound Station, Thence North forty-six degrees and fifteen minutes, East nine chains and twenty-five links to post No. 4 in Earth mound station—Thence South forty-three degrees and forty-five minutes East—"At sixteen links North corner Mission building bears South forty-six degrees and fifteen minutes West twenty links distant and one chain and twenty-one links to the place of beginning, containing one acre and twelve one (1 12/100) hundredths of an acre and designated upon the official plat of public surveys as Lot numbered Thirty-eight Township seven, North Range thirty-four West, S. B. M.

"Tract No. 3.—Old Church and Cemetery. "Beginning at East corner of Old Church at post No. 1 and running— "Thence South forty degrees and forty-five minutes West, the variation of the magnetic needle being fourteen degrees and fifteen minutes East—"At one chain and sixty-three links

MISSION
DE LA
PURISIMA

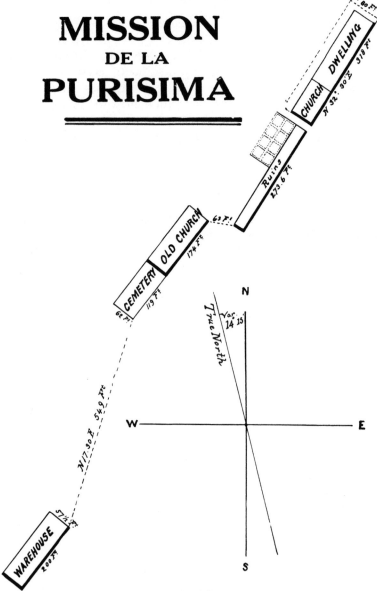

NOWHERE, AS IN PURISIMA, DID THE RAPACITY AND SAVAGENESS
OF THE PAISANO CHIEFS APPEAR SO EVIDENT.

corral fence course S. E. "At two chains and sixty-four links
corner of old Church Cemetery "At two chains and ninety-two
links corral fence course S. E. and four chains and seventy-
five links South corner cemetery and West corner corral to
post No. 2 station; Thence North fifty-one degrees West—
"At ninety-six links West corner, cemetery, at post No. 3,
Station—"Thence North forty degrees and forty-five minutes
East—"At two chains and eleven links North corner of Cemetery and four chains and seventy-five links to Post No. 4
in earth mound Station, Thence South fifty-one degrees East
"At forty-six links North corner old Church and ninety-six
links to the point of beginning containing forty-six (46/100)
one hundredths of an acre and designated upon the plat of
public surveys as lot numbered thirty-nine, Township seven
North Range thirty-four West—San Bernardino Meridian.

"Tract No. 4, Old Ware House—"Commencing at the East
corner of old ware House at a post—No. 1 "Thence the variation of the magnetic needle being fourteen degrees and fifty
minutes East-South fifty-two degrees West, three chains and
three links, to South corner old Ware House post marked No.
2 Station. "Thence North thirty-eight degrees West eighty-
eight links to west-corner old ware house post No. 3 Station.
"Thence North fifty-two degrees East three chains and three
links to North corner old Ware House post No. 4 Station.
"Thence South thirty-eight degrees East eighty-eight links to
the place of beginning containing twenty-seven one hundredths
of án acre (27/100) and designated upon the plat of public
surveys as lot numbered forty Township seven North Range
thirty-four West San Bernardino Base and Meridian—"Con-
necting Lines "Commencing at post No. 2 Tract No. 4 and
running "Thence South seventy-three degrees East "At
twelve chains forks of road course North, South and S. sixty-
five degrees East and touch point of hill on North East, course
South sixty-five degrees East and North twenty degrees
East—"At fourteen chains and twenty links post No. 6 Rancho
Mission La Purisima one hundred and twenty-three chains
and fifty links from south east corner of same."Commencing

at post No. 1, Tract No. 4 and thence running North thirty-one degrees East seven chains and eighty-nine links post No. 2 tract No. 3. "Commencing at a post No. 1 Tract No. 3 and then running North fifty-eight degrees East ninety-two links post No. 3, Tract No. 2, "Commencing at post No. 1, Tract No. 2 and then running North forty-three degrees East "At seven chains road course North and South and seven chains and ninety-eight links Station and—Thence North five degrees West thirty chains to post No. 1 Tract No. 1.

"In Testimony Whereof, I have signed my name officially and caused the seal of my office to be attached at the City of San Francisco, Cala, this 5th day of January A. D. 1874.

"J. R. HARDENBURGH

(L. S.)   "U. S. Surveyor General for Cala."

NOW KNOW YE, That the United States of America, in consideration of the premises and pursuant to the provisions of the Act of Congress aforesaid of 3d March, 1851, and the legislation supplemental thereto HAVE GIVEN and GRANTED and by these presents DO GIVE and GRANT unto the said JOSEPH S. ALEMANY, Bishop of Monterey, and to his successors, "in trust for the religious purposes and uses to which the same have been respectively, appropriated, the tracts of land embraced and described in the foregoing survey" but with the stipulation that in virtue of the 15th Section of the said Act, neither the confirmation of the claim nor this Patent shall affect the interests of third persons. To have and to hold the said tract with the appurtenances unto the said JOSEPH S. ALEMANY, Bishop of Monterey, and to his successors, in trust for the uses and purposes aforesaid, forever, with the stipulation aforesaid.

IN TESTIMONY WHEREOF, I ULYSSES S. GRANT, President of the United States have caused these LETTERS to be made PATENT and the Seal of the General Land Office to be hereunto affixed.

Given under my hand at the City of Washington this twenty-fourth day of January in the year of

our Lord One Thousand Eight Hundred and
Seventy-Four and of the Independence of the
United States the Ninety-Eight.

By the President: U. S. Grant,
(SEAL)   By S. D. Williamson, Secretary.

L. K. Lippincott, Recorder of the General Land Office.
Recorded Vol. 8 pp. 504 to 511 inclusive. Recorded at the
request of Ulpiano Yndart June 15th, A. D. 1874, at 9:40 A. M.

H. P. Stone, County Recorder.
By John C. Platt, Deputy.

STATE OF CALIFORNIA, ⎰ss.
County of Santa Barbara, ⎱

I, YRIS COVARRUBIAS, Recorder in and for the County
of Santa Barbara, do hereby certify the foregoing to be a full,
true and correct copy of the instrument appearing of record
in Book   A   of   Patents Page   177   Records
of Santa Barbara County, and that I have carefully compared
the same with the original record.

IN WITNESS WHEREOF, I have hereunto set
my hand and affixed my Official Seal, this
17th day of   June   , 1932.
(SEAL)   YRIS COVARRUBIAS, County Recorder,
By PAULINE GUTMAN, Deputy.

"The tracts of land embraced and described in the foregoing survey," granted "in trust for the religious purposes
and uses to which the same have been respectively appropriated," by sale came into the hands of seculars, as the following
Deed of Sale demonstrates:

FRANCIS MORA, BISHOP, & C. ⎱
to
EDUARDO DE LA CUESTA

THIS INDENTURE, made the 22nd day of January,
A. D., 1883,

Between Francis Mora Bishop of Monterey of the City and County of Los Angeles, State of California, a corporation sole, party of the first part and Eduardo de la Cuesta of the County of Santa Barbara, State of California, party of the second part,

WITNESSETH; That the said party of the first part for and in consideration of the sum of one dollar the receipt whereof is hereby acknowledged, has granted, bargained, sold and conveyed and confirmed and by these presents does grant, bargain, sell, convey and confirm unto the said party of the second part, and to his heirs and assigns forever, all that certain lot, piece or parcel of land lying and being situated in the County of Santa Barbara, State of California, and more particularly described as Tract No. One, Orchard as laid down on Plat of the Lands belonging to Mission de la Purisima, confirmed to J. S. Alemany, Bishop of Monterey &c approved January 24th, 1874, by Willis Drummond, commissioner of the General Land Office, which said map or plat is recorded in Book "A" of Patents pp. 177 to 181 on June 15th, 1874, and to which reference is hereby made.

"Tract No. 1 Orchard" Commencing at post No. 1 from which a pear tree ten inches in diameter (being the most westerly tree in the orchard) bears North sixty-four degrees East twenty-four links distant, Thence the variation of the magnetic needle being fourteen degrees and fifteen minutes East, North thirty-seven degrees and fifteen minutes East, at seven chains and fifty links centre of reservoir fifty links in diameter bears South fifty degrees East two hundred links distant, at eight chains and five links, an old aqueduct course South East and ascends at ten chains and fifty-four links fence near its north corner course South East and thirteen chains and twenty-one links to Post No. 2, earth mound Station, Thence descending South fifty-two degrees and thirty minutes East, At six chains enter valley course East and West, At nine chains and nineteen links a post marked No. 3, Station, a willow tree twelve inches in diameter bears North fifty-one degrees West two chains and forty-two links distant,

and remainders, rents, issues and profits thereof. And also all the estate, right, title, interest, property, possession, claim and demand whatsoever as well in law as in equity, of the said party of the first part of, in or to the said premises and every part and parcel thereof with the appurtenances.

To have and to hold all and singular the said premises together with the appurtenances, unto the said party of the second part and to his heirs and assigns forever.

In Witness Whereof the said party of the first part has hereunto set his hand and seal the day and year first above written.

FRANCIS MORA, R. C. Bishop of Monterey,

(CORPORATE SEAL)

Sole Corporation

Signed, sealed and delivered
in the presence of A. C. Holmes.

State of California   ⎱
County of Los Angeles ⎰ ss.

On this 22d day of January one thousand eight hundred and eighty-three, before me, A. C. Holmes, a Notary Public, in and for the County of Los Angeles, personally appeared Francis Mora, the Roman Catholic Bishop of Monterey, personally known to me to be the same person described in, whose name is subscribed to the within instrument, and known to me to be the Bishop of Monterey, a corporation sole, acknowledged to me that he executed the same.

In Witness Whereof, I have hereunto set my hand and affixed my official seal, the day and year in this certificate first above written.

(NOTARIAL SEAL)   A. C. HOLMES, Notary Public

Recorded at the request of R. de la Cuesta January 29th, 1883, at 50 minutes past 10 o'clock A. M.

A. B. WILLIAMS, Recorder,
By Harry Goodchild, Deputy Recorder.

STATE OF CALIFORNIA ⎱
  County of Santa Barbara, ⎰ ss.

I, YRIS COVARRUBIAS, Recorder in and for the County of Santa Barbara, do hereby certify the foregoing to be a full, true and correct copy of the instrument appearing of record in Book   1   of   Deeds Page   386   Records of Santa Barbara County, and that I have carefully compared the same with the original record.

IN WITNESS WHEREOF, I have hereunto set my hand and affixed my Official Seal, this   17th (SEAL)   day of   June,   1932.

YRIS COVARRUBIAS, County Recorder,
By PAULINE GUTMAN, Deputy.

CHAPTER IX.

The Records of Mission Purisima Concepción, folio size and bound in flexible leather covers, still existed at Mission Santa Inés till 1925. They consist of the Baptismal Register in two volumes, the Marriage Register in one volume, the Burial Register in two volumes, and the Confirmation Register in one volume, besides a Padron. At Mission Santa Barbara are the Account Books to the year 1824, and various Padrons, or Registers of the neophytes by families, with additions for single men, widowers and their children, single women, widows and their children, and orphaned children, from the year 1799 to 1836.

Much interesting information might be extracted from these priceless voumes; but, as the statistical material has been collected in the Tables we shall confine ourselves here to reproducing the chief incidents not already stated.

It will be observed on glancing at the Table of the Spiritual Results of the Mission activity that from the very beginning applications for admission to the Mission fold were quite numerous, and the average for twelve years preceding the close of the eighteenth century being 108 converts a year. This gratified the hearts of the zealous missionaries, but it also entailed much additional labor, as all over nine years of age had to be instructed in the rudiments of the Christian Faith, and the elders had to be put on probation besides in order to insure against relapse into paganism. Usually the women and girl candidates were taught the catechism apart from the men. The children also had their own hours for instruction. A general recitation of what had been learned or was to be learned and observed took place every morning in the church during holy Mass, and in the evening at a suitable hour. All recited aloud, and thus new-comers with no difficulty learned by heart the whole *Doctrina* from merely hearing it recited every day. Hymns in both Latin and Spanish would be sung, especially in the evening, or while at work when the mood was on the converts. The Rosary, too was recited in common. As it merely consisted of the Lord's Prayer, the Hail Mary, and the Doxology, these were acquired without difficulty by the most obtuse mind through repetition. The beautiful Salve Regina and the Litany were sung, especially during the processions. The *Alabado*, this peculiarly Spanish praise of the Blessed Sacrament and of the Immaculate Queen, would generally close the devotions. The daily routine in this and other respect was uniformly observed in all the Missions. Thus the Indians became so used to the prayers and hymns, and they were so firmly grounded by practice on the doctrinal and moral points of Religion, that even after half a century, when no priests had appeared among the descendants of the Mission Indians away from the cities and ranchos, they recited all that their fathers and mothers had learned and practiced. Hence it was that they preserved the priceless treasure of Christian Faith, even when, for lack of guidance and moral support, they lapsed into a wild life.

The first converts and missionaries have already been named. Fr. Lasuén, the aged founder, and the Superior of the Franciscans in California, visited Purisima a second time just three years after the founding, December 8, 1790, the titular feast of the Mission. He arrived from Mission San Luis Obispo that morning at 8 o'clock, and found that already 288 names of neophytes had been entered in the baptismal register. The celebration for the morning having terminated, Fr. Lasuén in the afternoon baptised an Indian girl of ten years, to whom he applied the name of the Mission's Patroness, Maria Concepta. Immediately after he also conferred upon her the Sacrament of Confirmation.

Next day which was made a holyday; Fr. Lasuén still vested in his sacerdotal robes as at holy Mass, except the chasuble, gave an instruction to the assembled neophytes and a few whites on the Sacrament of Confirmation. First he informed them that only a Bishop could ordinarily administer this Sacrament; but that, owing to the lack of a Bishop in the whole territory, the Holy Father in Rome had empowered him to administer Confirmation, with the Holy Oils blessed by the Bishop of Sonora, the Ordinary of the diocese to which California belonged. Fr. Lasuén then instructed the candidates with regard to the conditions and dispositions for receiving the Sacrament worthily. All were also told that Confirmation could be received but once. Thereupon, assisted by Fathers Arroita and Orámas, the resident missionaries, and by Fr. José Calzada of Mission San Gabriel, he confirmed 74 persons entered as Nos. 2 to 75. On December the 10th, after holy Mass, Nos. 76 to 85; on December 11, Nos. 86 to 93; and finally on December 12, after holy Mass, Nos. 94 to 263, including soldiers and their families. Every one confirmed had his or her sponsor, who was informed of the relationship contracted. Fathers Arroita and Orámas signed their names at the end of the list of those confirmed.

In the following year, June 24 and 26, 1791, Fr. Lasuén confirmed Nos. 264 to 343. On October 19 and 20, Fr. Lasuén administered Confirmation to Nos. 344 to 560. This time Fr. Calzada signed with Fr. Arroita, Fr. Orámas having been transferred to Mission San Gabriel. Fr. Lasuén returning from his visitation to the south, on May 4, 1794, confirmed Nos. 561 to 578, who had been prepared. Coming from the north in September, Fr. Lasuén first baptised, on September 20, thirty-nine Indian adults, and then confirmed them together with a child. Next day, September 21, he confirmed sixteen more neophytes. The zealous Fr. Presidente returned from the south, and on November 16, 1794, confirmed Nos. 637 to 689. It was the last time; for, although he visited Purisima in August, 1797, his authority to confirm granted for only ten years, expired in May, 1795. The Sacrament of Confirmation was not again conferred at Purisima Concepción till the arrival of the first Bishop. Although the Bishop came in December 1841, he did not visit Purisima till May 7, 1844.

He then confirmed Nos. 690 to 712. There is no record that at any time thereafter Confirmation was administered here.

Shortly before Fr. Lasuén's second Confirmation visit March 29, 1791, Fr. Orámas penned the following interesting note in the baptismal register: "We were informed that in the rancherias of Estayt and Sisolop were some people critically ill. Casimiro, the Indian interpreter, being well instructed in the method of catechising and instructing those who wanted to receive holy Baptism, and also in the form and everything else requisite for the (private) administration of the Sacrament, and we missionaries being unable to succor these sick people spiritually, directed the said Casimiro to ask them whether they wanted to become Christians. If he discovered that they desired it, he should instruct them and baptise them. On the following day Casimiro returned and said that in the rancheria of Estayt he had baptised a male Indian sixty years of age, who was in the last stage of disease, also a boy of eight years in the same extremity; and in the rancheria of Sisolop a boy of four years in the same extremity."

During the years 1794-1796 a great many Indians joined the Mission, and in consequence, after receiving the requisite instruction, frequently large numbers would be assembled for Baptism. Fr. Lasuén himself as we have seen, baptised forty adults on one day in September, 1794. The first thousand was reached in May, 1797, only nine years after the founding of the Mission. Exceedingly large numbers of converts were admitted in 1803-1804. The former year was a banner year for Baptisms here, 451 Indians, mostly over nine years of age, having been regenerated during the twelve months.

A great many pagans left their mountain haunts, and joined the Mission in that year 1812, the year of the earthquake, but previous to the disaster. Among them, on November 14, 1812, was the chief named Neuia, who counted about 60 summers. Two weeks after the earthquake, January 3, 1813, Fr. Payéras baptised 74 Indian adults and one child, (Nos. 2536-2611) in the much damaged church. One would think that the calamity had frightened all the neophytes away from the Mission. It seems to have had the opposite effect.

The last Baptisms in the ruined church building were administered by Fr. Payéras on April 10, 1813, nearly four months after the earthquake. They were Nos. 2630-2631. The last was a child. This number then was reached at the site of the first Mission, Lompoc. Immediately after this entry Fr. Ripoll made the following remark: "First Baptism (i. e. No. 2632), which was administered in the new Mission, the transfer of which took place on April 23, 1813." The subject was an Indian male infant to whom the name Ivon was given. The date was April 29, 1813.

Fr. Luis Gil, who for the first time officiated on June 1, 1813, had a big draft as fisher of men on August 5, 1815, when he baptised Nos. 2764-2826, sixty-three in all, 22 of whom were children. In addition on the same happy day Fr. Gil supplied the ceremonies for one baptised in *articulo mortis*, but who apparently had recovered. Such days, although very hard on the missionary, counted among the happy ones of the priests life.

Fr. Vincente de Sarría, accompanied by Fr. Estévan Tápis as secretary, arrived at the Mission Purisima for the first time on September 18, 1813, and left his auto-de-visita on the front fly leaf as was his custom. He made the next visitation together with Fr. Antonio Rodríguez as secretary, on June 27, 1816. His third and last visit occured in company of Fr. Jayme Escude, on June 23, 1818, when he was succeeded as Commissary Prefect by Fr. Mariano Payéras, who made Mission Purisima his headquarters.

The first Book of Baptisms was filled up by October 8, 1834, when Fr. Marcos Antonio de Vitoria entered No. 3283. The volume closes with the following note in the hand of Fr. Felipe Arroyo de la Cuesta on September 23, 1834: "Hence the first entry of the second Book of Baptisms of this said Mission must be No. 3288, because this first book has concluded with the number 3287, as noted above, and will be seen.

Although on the present occasion there *are not at this mission*, the Rev. Preachers Apostolic and Missionaries, who have been the last of it (i. e. of the Mission), because our immediate Prelate, the Rev. Fr. Presidente Fr. Narciso Durán, has so disposed on account of the circumstances of the times; nevertheless, it has appeared to me well to proceed thus, constrained by the reasons, which I have pointed out in this note.—Fr. Felipe Arroyo."

The page closed with this line from I Timothy i, 17: "Soli Deo honor et Gloria in saeculorum, Amen."—"To God alone be honor and glory forever and ever, Amen."

From this it is clear that Fr. Durán, immediately after the "secularition" in 1834, had instructed Fr. Vitoria, the priest in charge, and Fr. Arroyo, who had come down from Mission San Juan Bautista, and was a cripple, to retire to Mission Santa Inés, and to attend Mission Purisima in spiritual matters from there. Fr. Arroyo, methodical as ever, now led a list of missionaries, whose names appear in the baptismal register, follow. There were thirty-two. He omitted himself, however. So there were actually thirty-three missionaries in the history of Purisima Concepción, down to 1834. Fr. Ramon Abella, who came in July, 1836, and Fr. Francisco Sánchez and the Rev. Miguel Gómez may be added, as they come in before 1846.

It is also of interest that down to October, 1834, when the first Book of Baptism closed, only thirty-eight white people had been baptised here, whereas the number of Indian Baptisms ran up to 2,345.

The few surviving Indians seem to have brought their Children for Baptism to Mission Santa Inés. At all events, the phrase "en la iglesia de esta Mision de la Purisima Concepción," was used for the last time by Fr. Arroyo de la Cuesta in connection with No. 3338 on March 30, 1836, the subject being a child from the Rancho San Antonio named Cornelia. Thereafter the entries always read "en la iglesia de esta Mision," then "en la capilla publica de esta Mision," or "en la iglesia de esta Mision," doubtless Santa Inés was meant,

RIFT IN THE MOUNTAINS BACK OF THE MISSION AT LOMPOC. A CONTEMPORARY FLOOD WASHED OUT THE SOIL AND SPREAD IT ALL OVER THE DOOMED MISSION.

where the Fathers resided. Fr. Abella is the last one to use the term "en la iglesia," on July 25, 1836, with No. 3339. It is doubtful whether after that date divine service was held at the ruined Mission. The Rev. Doroteo Ambris in an entry of February 2, 1846, in the second volume of Baptisms of Purisima Mission Indians, writes "en la Capilla publica de esta Mision," which without doubt was the chapel at the seminary of Santa Inés.

Fr. Francisco Sánchez, the *Fr. Salvadierra* in Mrs. H. H. Jackson's Ramona, was the last Franciscan to enter a Baptism in the Purisima Book. This happened on February 2, 1850, the subject being Francisca. Then follows in a fine hand the Rev. Eugene O'Connell with this remark: "La continuacion de este Libro se halla en el de la Mision the Santa Inés, V. y M., unidas las partidas de una y otra."—The continuation of this book is in the one of Mission Santa Inés, Virgin and Martyr, with the entries of the one and the other."

BURIAL REGISTER

The title page to the Burial Register, or Libro de los Entierros, was written by Fr. Presidente Lasuén, and is like that of the Baptisms and Marriages, barring the change of the word Burial for Baptism.

The first entry was made by Fr. Fuster on February 14, 1789, more than a year after the founding of the Mission. The subject was Juana de la Cruz, the child of an Indian neophyte.

The most interesting information in the volume is entry No. 2197, of April 29, 1823, which commemorates the death of Fr. Mariano Payéras. It will be reproduced in connection with his biographical sketch.

Then come entries of the burial of the victims in the revolt of February and March, 1824, which happily good Fr. Payéras did not live to bewail. They have been already reproduced in connection with the narrative on the uprising. The entries, in the case of the Indians, give the number each held in the baptismal register also.

The last entry in the first Book of Burials is by Fr. Vitoria. It is No. 2549, and the date is December 29, 1831. Of these 2549 burials 1518 had occurred on the first Mission site, Lompoc.

As in the case of the baptismal register, the methodical, though crippled, Fr. Arroyo de la Cuesta enumerates the Fathers who had officiated at burials, and adds their native country. There were twenty-one Franciscan Fathers down to the end of 1831, when the first volume closes. From this we see that the Fathers hailed: two from Catalonia, six from Cantabria, two from Aragon, two from Burgos, four from Mayorca, one from Estremadura, two from Mexico, and two from Cuba. Those of the Fathers, who had died by that time, 1831, were marked in the list with a cross before the name.

The second Book of Burials begins with the entry of No. 2550 by Fr. Vitoria, on January 13, 1832. The entry was written by Fr. Arroyo, but signed by Fr. Vitoria. This happened frequently, as Fr. Arroyo could do nothing else save labor with his hands. Later on he seems to have grown somewhat stronger, so that he could officiate for nearly a year, October 1835 to July 3, 1836. This latter was his last entry, but made at Mission Santa Inés. It reads as follows: "No. 2747. En el Cementerio de esta Iglesia de la Purisima, el Sacristano Gregorio Alejo y otros individuous enterraron a Ivon, soltero, su partida (in the Baptismal Register) 2632. Recibió los Sacramentos de Penitencia y Extrema Uncion, y murio el dia anterior."

An important note was entered in the burial register by Fr. Juan Moreno, who wrote: "The following entries are of these who died in the epidemic of small pox. There are but very few who died without Confession and the other Sacraments. All these have died at the Mission at Los Alamos, in the Tulares, and in the mountain regions. Hence the entries cannot be made with due accuracy, wherefore I give only the names, the Sacraments, and the burial, from July of the present year till November." Then Fr. Moreno proceeds to make the entries of Nos. 2910-2964, and signs the list but once, not after each entry as is the rule. This must have occurred in November 1844. No date is specified, but it is clear that the epidemic started in July, 1844. The dead were mostly adults.

The last entry of a Franciscan was that of Fr. Francisco Sánchez, and dated April 24, 1850. Thereafter only one entry was made by the Rev. Theodosius Boussier and one by the Rev. Eugene O'Connell.

MARRIAGE REGISTER

The title page by Fr. Lasuén reads the same as that of the Baptismal Register, barring the substitution of the word Marriage for Baptism. The first entry was that of an Indian neophyte couple, which after their Baptism merely renewed their consent before the Fr. Vincente Fuster on the eve of Pentecost Sunday, May 10, 1788, and then received the marriage blessing. Their names were Mariano Tamolechet and Maria Concepcion.

The last entry of a Franciscan was No. 1097, by Fr. José Joaquin Jimeno, and dated October 7, 1849. Thereafter only once more an entry was made in October, 1851, by the Rev. Amable Petithomme.

As in the case of the other registers, Fr. Arroyo de la Cuesta appended a list of all the Fathers whose names appear in the book.

CHAPTER X.

Nothing is known of the antecedents of *Fr. Francisco de Arroita*, except that he came from the Spanish province of Cantabria, and joined the missionary College of San Fernando de Mexico in 1784. In a letter of Fr. Guardian Sancho, dated April 1, 1786, Fr. Presidente Lasuén was notified that Fr. Arroíta was proceeding to California in the company of five other Franciscan Fathers. They were Fr. Faustino Solá, Pasqual Arenaza, Norberto Santiago, "countrymen of Your Reverence," the Fr. Guardian remarks, besides Fr. Hilário Torrent and Cristóbal Orámas. They probably landed at Monterey in September, 1786. At all events, Fr. Arroíta baptised at San Carlos on September 8, 1786, signing Fr. Josef, not José, or Joseph. Fr. Lasuén assigned him to Mission San Luis Obispo, where he baptised for the first time on April 7, 1787, and for the last time on February 5, 1788. While here he made a visit to San Carlos and baptised there once on October 21, 1787. From Mission San Luis Obispo, Fr. Arroíta was appointed one of the two founders of Mission Purisima Concepción. He arrived on the ground in April 1788, and on the 9th of that month administered Baptism at one of the rancherias to an adult Indian who was *in articulo mortis*.

Fr. Arroíta would occasionally visit Mission San Luis Obispo, and then he would be asked to officiate. Hence we find his name in the Baptismal Register on October 8, 1788, November 4, 1791, August 8, 1792, June 18, 1794, and September 27 and 29, 1794. At Santa Barbara his name appears in the Baptismal Book on October 12, 1791, December 2, 1792, April 18 and 19, 1793, and November 25, 1794. He also was present there at the death of Fr. Antonio Paterna, the first missionary of Santa Barbara Mission, February 13, 1793.

Fr. Arroíta continued to serve at Purisima until June 21, 1796, when he entered his last Baptism. On July 20, Fr.

Presidente Lasuén notified Governor Diego de Borica that he had given Fr. Arroíta permission to retire to the College, as he had completed his teim of ten years in California, and was worn out from the hardships endured. He sailed for San Blas, and on reaching San Fernando lived there until midnight of March 5, 1821, when he passed to eternal rest.

Under date of January 24, 1794, Fr. Thomas de Pangua, Guardian of the College of San Fernando de Mexico, informed Fr. Lasuén, that he had selected five Fathers of the College who would be to his satisfaction in the Missions of California. "They are, he wrote, Fr. Gregório Fernández of the Province of Burgos, 40 years of age, of which he had passed 22 in the Order, of robust health and good conduct, who came to the College in 1785. Fr. Josef Martiaiena, Fr. Manuel Fernández, Fr. Josef Estéban, and Fr. Juan Martín. They were only waiting for means to defray the expenses of the journey. Fr. Gregório was born in 1754, and he entered the Franciscan Order in 1772. It seems the Fathers landed at San Francisco, for under date of June 23, 1794, Fr. Gregório Fernández baptized at Dolores. One of his companions, Fr. Juan Martín, also baptized there, although more than a month later. He was appointed for Mission San Luis Obispo, and for the first time officiated at a Baptism on July 29, 1794. His last entry there is dated July 2, 1796. He was next assigned to Mission Purisima Concepción, where he baptized for the first time on May 22, 1796. He had paid a visit to the place before, as his name appears in the Register on September 21, 1794.

On August 4, 1804, Fr. Presidente Tápis notified the Fr. Guardian that Fr. Gregório would retire from California to the College. Fr. Fernández accordingly appears for the last time in the Baptismal Register on September 21, 1805.

While stationed at Purisima, Fr. Gregório visited San Luis Obispo at least once, and baptized there on August 19, 1804. From May 24-28, 1800, he officiated at Baptisms at Mission Santa Barbara.

"Fr. Fernández," says Bancroft, "was styled *un angel* (an angel) when he came to California; and there is nothing to

show that his angelic qualities deteriorated in California."
Fr. Gregório sailed for Mexico on November 6, 1805. He had
served his ten years, and was entitled to retire to the College.

Concerning Fr. *Mariano Payéras* we have details from the
best authority of the territory—Fr. Vicente de Sarría, the
Commissary Prefect of California, and the highest superior
of the Franciscans at the time. In his biographical sketches
of the Fathers of his time, Fr. Sarría in November 1817, writes
of Fr. Payéras as follows: "Fr. Mariano Payéras, forty-seven
years of age, is a native of the Villa de Inca, Isle of Mayorca.
He received the habit in the Convento Grande of Our Father
Saint Francis at Palma on September 5, 1784. In January,
1793, he left his native province for the Apostolic College of
San Francisco de Mexico, where he remained two years and
some months in the exercise of the duties of the institution."

"In 1796 he was sent to these Missions of Upper California.
All the Missions which he served can present evidence of his
wonderful zeal. These Missions are those of San Carlos, Our
Lady of Soledad, San Diego with its immediate presidio, and
lastly Purisima Concepción, which he has administered since
1804. However, confining myself entirely to more recent
times, in which, owing to my office and inspection, I have
come in touch with him, and have learnt to know in visitations
and outside of them so that I am qualified to attest with some
knowledge and likelihood I regard his merit as exceptional
and distinguished, for his genius as a religious as well as an
industrious and successful manager, which he displays in the
conduct of his own Mission. Likewise, since he has been
named in July, 1815, by the Venerable Discretory Presidente
of these Missions, he has laudably discharged the functions,
which by virtue of the office or by special commission especially
of the Bishop belong to him in behalf of the people called de
Razon. His disposition fits him for other offices especially for
such as are somewhat analogous to the ministry that has been
entrusted to him."

No higher recommendation could have been given to a
missionary. Fr. Sarría actually lets the College understand

that Fr. Payéras was suitable for the office of Commisary Prefect, the highest in the territory.

So, when Fr. Sarría's term of six years expired in 1819, we need not wonder to find the College of San Fernando name Fr. Mariano to succeed him as Commissary Prefect for California.

From the biographical sketches of the Fathers, which Fr. Payéras in turn issued on December 31, 1820, he writes of himself that he was then fifty-one years of age; that he had joined the College in 1793; that he had there for three years been preaching Missions to the faithful and had been active in other labors common to the apostolic ministry; that in 1796 he had come to the California Missions; that for the last five years he had been Presidente of the Fathers and Vicar of the Bishop; and that since October 1819, he was Comisário Prefecto.

Fr. Payéras probably landed at Monterey in the beginning of July, 1796. San Carlos was his first missionary field. He began to officiate at Baptisms on July 10, the subject being number 2121 in the Records of Baptisms. His last entry is dated September 7, 1798. He was then appointed for Our Lady de Soledad Mission, where he baptized for the first time on November 17, 1798. He remained there till about the end of August, 1803, baptizing for the last time on the 23rd. During this period he visited Mission San Miguel once, and baptized there on December 15 and 19, 1800; and Mission Santa Clara once, as he baptized there on July 7, 1801. Fr. Payéras was now transferred to Mission San Diego. He officiated there at a Baptism for the first time on December 11, 1803. As we do not find his name in any of the Mission Registers south of Soledad, we presume he made the voyage by ship from Monterey. At Mission San Diego Fr. Payéras remained till the beginning of October, 1804, having baptized there for the last time on September 30th. Finally he received Mission Purisima Concepción as his next and last field of labor. He began officiating at Baptisms on November 3, 1804.

It was No. 2,100 in the Book. Hence before his arrival 2,198 Baptisms had been administered at this Mission.

In July, 1815, the College of San Fernando appointed Fr. Mariano Presidente of the Franciscans in California, to succeed Fr. José Senan of Mission San Buenaventura. In this capacity he had to attend to the purely religious affairs of the friars, subject to the Commissary Prefect, Fr. Vicente de Sarría, who acted as a kind of perpetual visitor general, subject to the Commissary General in Mexico. In ecclesiastical affairs, however, Fr. Mariano Payéras was the head of the Church in the territory as representative or Vicar of the Bishop of Sonora. All extending of faculities and dispensations, etc., for the people had to be arranged by him. He held this office until the expiration of Fr. Sarría's six year term as Commissary Prefect. In October, 1819, Fr. Mariano was promoted to the office vacated by Fr. Sarría. His duties now necessitated making the visitation of the Missions and of their ministers. Leaving Mission Purisima in charge of Fr. Antonio Rodríguez, Fr. Payéras set out for San Carlos and began his Visitations there on August 31, 1820. Thereupon he visited the Missions to the north, in the following order: San Juan Bautista, Santa Cruz, Santa Clara, San Francisco, San José, and San Raphael, the latter on October 21, 1820. He then returned to Mission Purisima. He resumed the visitations in the next year, beginning at Mission San Antonio on June 14, 1821, and then made the visitations at all the Missions to the southward, until he reached Mission San Diego and viseed the books on August 29, 1821. In all these Missions he left a certificate of the visitation, or of the Auto-de-Visita, in all the Registers. It was always countersigned by a Father who acted as secretary and so styled himself. Fr. José Bernardo Sanchez accompanied him on the journey of the year 1821 as secretary.

While at San Diego, the zealous Fr. Commissary Payéras resolved to visit the country to the east of the southern Mission with a view to finding suitable sites for new Missions; for it grieved him to see the Indians of the interior from the San

Diego District to the Tulares outside the pale of Christianity. Although he could not tell whence to secure either missionaries or means, he insisted on surveying the territory. Accompanied by Fr. José Sanchez, who left us a diary of the journey, Fr. Payéras set out from Mission San Diego on September 10, 1821, and scoured the whole country, planted a cross at Santa Isabél, and he made a stop at Pala, a Mission station or asistencia of Mission San Luis Rey. On September 23 he resumed his journey to the northeast as far as San Jacinto and then with Fr. Sanchez made his way to Mission San Gabriel, which after many hardships was reached in the evening of October 1, 1821. Details the reader will find in volumes on the Missions of San Diego and San Luis Rey. It is not possible here to relate all that the zealous Fr. Commissary accomplished or attempted to accomplish. The reader will find all in the volume iii of *The Missions and Missionaries*.

Fr. Payéras in October, 1822, accompanied the imperial commissioner, Rev. Agustin Fernandez, on his trip to the Russian settlement at Fort Ross. Leaving Monterey on October 11, the little company proceeded, crossing San Francisco Bay, and reached Mission San Rafael on the 19th. On the next day, a Sunday, Fr. Payéras celebrated the High Mass. The journey was continued till Fort Ross was reached on October 23. From there the return march was made, and continued until all arrived at Mission San Juan Bautista on November 2. Fr. Payéras kept a *diário* of the trip which is still extant. The hardships suffered on the trip while not well, doubtless accelerated his death, which occurred at his beloved Purisima on April 28, 1823, at the age of only fifty-three years, seven months, and eighteen days. His last Baptisms at Purisima were Nos. 3102-3103, on March 5, 1823. The Burial entry reads as follows:

"No. 2197. On the 29th day of April, 1823, in the church of this Mission of Purisima, I gave ecclesiastical burial to the body of the Very Rev. Fr. Mariano Payéras, Preacher Apostolic of the College of San Fernando de Mexico, missionary of the said Mission, and actual Prefect of these Missions. He received the holy habit in the Province of Mayorca. He died on the preceding day, disposing himself for this terrible ordeal with religious and exemplary edification to the Fathers as well as for the people *de razon* and the neophytes. He is buried under the pulpit of said church, and he received all the holy Sacraments. In witness whereof I sign this.—Fr. Antonio Rodríguez."

"There was no missionary with whose public life and character for the past eight years the reader is better acquainted than with that of Fr. Payéras," writes Bancroft. "There was no friar of better and more even balanced ability in the province. He was personally a popular man on account of his affable manners, kindness of heart, and unselfish devotion to the welfare of all. It was impossible to quarrel with him, and even Governor Sola's peevish and annoying complaints never ruffled his temper. Yet he had extraordinary business ability, was a clear and forcible as well as a voluminous writer, and withal a man of great strength of mind and firmness of character. He was called to rule the friars during a trying period, when it would have required but a trifle to involve the padres and soldiers in a quarrel fatal to the missions. His death just at this time, in the prime of life, must be considered as a great misfortune."

Bancroft could write nice things about the Franciscans if he wanted to.

FRANCISCANS STATIONED OR VISITING AT PURISIMA CONCEPCION

Fr. Fermin Francisco de Lasuén, Founder.

Fr. Vicente Fustér, April 8, 1788, to August 15, 1789. First Baptism No. 2; last, No. 147.

Fr. Joseph Arroíta, April 8, 1788, to June 21, 1796.

Fr. Cristóbal Orámas, August 7-9, 1788, Nos. 63-70.

Fr. José Cavaller, August 10, 1788, Nos. 72-79.

Fr. Miguel Giribet, May 14, 1789, Nos. 111-118.

Fr. Cristóbal Orámas, first No. 152, December 28, 1789; last No. 589, November 2, 1792.

Fr. José de Miguel, No. 254, August 25, 1790.

Fr Lasuén, No. 289, December 8, 1790.

Fr. Estévan Tápis, Nos. 353-355, March 19-20; March 22, 1791, No. 357.

Fr. Lasuén, Nos. 390-400, June 23, 1791.

Fr. José de Miguel, October 22, 1791, Nos. 458-459; April 27, No. 526, 1792.

Fr. Miguel Pieras, No. 479, December, 1791.

Fr. Giribet, December 10, 1791; October 8 and 16, 1792.

Fr. Jose Ant. Calzada, first Nos. 592-593, November 22, 1792; No. 973, July 4, 1796.

Fr. Tápis, Nos. 619-622, March 30, 1793; No. 681, May 11, 1794.

Fr. Lasuén, Nos. 699-738, all adults, September 20, 1794.

Fr. Gregório Fernández, No. 739, September 21, 1794.

Fr. José de Miguel, February 7, March 20, 1795; February 5, 1796; June 1796 and 1797.

Fr. Giribet, April 3, 1796, Nos. 951-952.

Fr. Gregório Fernández, first, No. 965, May 22, 1796; last September 21, 1805, No. 2302.

Fr. Juan Martín, May 28, September 11, 1796; July 11, August 6, 1797.

Fr. Joseph Panella, No. 1005, May 14, 1797.

Fr. Antonio Peyri, July 11, 1797, No. 1012.

Fr. Lasuén, Nos. 1015-1016, August 16, 1797.

Fr. Francisco X. Uría, first, No. 1021, October 2, 1797; last July 26, 1798, No. 1190.

Fr. Pedro de San Josef Estevan, Nos. 1026-1042, October 17, 1797, adults.

Fr. José Manuel de Martiarena, May 20, June 20, 1798.

Fr. Ant. Peyri, April 29, 1798, Nos. 1162-1164.

Fr. José Ant. Calzada, first, September 2, 1798, Nos. 1194-1196; last August 25, 1804.

Fr. Tápis, April 30, 1800, Nos. 1322-1323.

Fr. Juan Cortes, Nos. 1361-1362, September 6, 1800.

Fr. José de Miguel, September 7, 1801; May 23, 25, September 8, 1802; May 14, 1803.

Fr. Juan Cortéz, September 4, Nos. 1529-1530; September 8, 1802, Nos. 1534-1536.

Fr. Pedro Adriano Martinez, Nos. 1515-1517, July 6, 1802.

Fr. Romualdo Gutiérrez, No. 2191, September 9, 1804.

Fr. José de Miguel, September 10, 1803, Nos. 1810-1826, adults.

Fr. P. A. Martinez, Nos. 1827-1841, September 10, 1803, adults.

Fr. Mariano Payéras, first, No. 2199, November 3, 1804.

Fr. Juan Cabot, No. 2306, October 31, 1805.

Fr. Gerónimo Boscana, first, No. 2357, December 10, 1806; last May 5, 1811.

Fr. Estévan Tápis, first No. 2521, September 4, 1811; last No. 2548, August 14, 1812.

Fr. Antonio Ripoll, first, September 14, 1812, No. 2550; last May 1, 1815, No. 2757.

Fr. Luis y Taboada, first, June 1, 1815, No. 2759; last, October 29, 1817, No. 2956.

Fr. Luis Ant. Martinez, No. 2947, July 26, 1817.

Fr. Roman Ulibarri, first, October 15, 1818, No. 2983; last July 3, 1819, No. 3013.

Fr. Antonio Rodríguez, September 12, 1819, Nos. 3015; last No. 3025, February 2, 1820.

Fr. Vincente Pasqual Oliva, April, 13-14, May 2, 7, 1820; June 11, 1819.

Fr. José Sanchez, first, July 2, 1820, No. 3031; last, November 28, 1821, No. 3074.

Fr. Antonio Rodríguez, first, No. 3053, March 2, 1821; last September 20, 1824, No. 3139.

Fr. Blas Ordáz, April 13, 1823, No. 3104, February 8, to March 25, 1824.

Fr. Marcos Antonio de Vitoria, first, No. 3140, December 18, 1824; last, June 19, 1835, No. 3334.

Fr. José Joaquin Jimeno, No. 3213, December 29, 1829.

Fr. Juan Moreno, September 12, October 15, 1834, No. 3277; last September 6, 1835.

Fr. Felipe Arroyo de la Cuesta, September 23, 1834, with No. 3287, begins to enter though Fr. Vitoria signs them. Last, March 30, 1836, No. 3338.

Fr. J. J. Jimeno, first, January 10, 1836, No. 3335.

Fr. Ramon Abella, July 25, 1836, December 9, 1839, January, 1842, No. 3365.

Fr. Francisco Sanchez, April 20, 1842, July 9, 1844.

Rev. José Miguel Gómez, October 15, 1842; February 19, March 5, 1843.

Rev. Doroteo Ambris, February 2, 1846, No. 3384.

Secular Priests or resident rectors of the Parish of the Immaculate Conception at Lompoc, California, according to the Catholic Directory.

Rev. John Reynolds, 1911-1912, April.

Rev. Charles Raley, July, 1912-1918, May.

Rev. Francis Woodcutter, June, 1918-March, 1919.

Rev. Thomas B. Morris, March, 1919-December, 1920.

Rev. John Morgan, January, 1921-November, 1922.

Rev. J. B. Roure, November, 1922-January, 1929.

Rev Peter C. Santy, January, 1929-July, 1930.

Rev. Timothy O'Shea, October, 1930-

CHAPTER XI.

After the devoted missionaries and their Indian neophytes, through force of the circumstances noted in the narrative, had abandoned their beloved home, the buildings decayed rapidly. Mrs. Helen Hunt Jackson, as United States Indian Inspector, in 1882 viewed the ruins, and in her *Glimpses of California and the Missions* (pages 93-94) graphically described what she witnessed as follows: "The most desolate ruin of all is that of La Purisima Mission. Nothing is left there but one long, low adobe building, with a few arches of the corridor; the door stands wide open, the roof is falling in; it has been so often used as a stable and sheepfold, that even the grasses are killed around it. The painted pulpit hangs half falling on the wall, its stairs are gone, and its sounding-board is slanting awry. Inside the broken altar-rail is a pile of stones, earth, and rubbish thrown up by seekers after buried treasures; in the farther corner another pile and hole, the home of a badger; mud swallows' nest are thick on the cornice, and cobwebbed rags of the old canvas ceiling hang fluttering overhead. The only trace of the ancient cultivation is a pear-orchard a few rods off, which must have been a splended sight in its day; it is at least two hundred yards square, with a double row of trees all around, so placed as to leave between them a walk fifty or sixty feet wide. Bits of broken aqueduct here and there, and a large, round stone tank overgrown by grass, showed where the life of the orchard used to flow in. It has been many years slowly dying of thirst. Many of the trees are gone, and those that remain stretch out gaunt and shrivelled boughs, which, though still bearing fruit, look like arms tossing in vain reproach and entreaty; a few pinched little blossoms seemed to heighten rather than lessen their melancholy look."

Mr. George Wharton James, the noted author of *In And Out Of The Old Missions*, (207-209) twenty-three years later wrote as follows on what he observed: "The Mission of La Purisima Concepción was built in a cañada not far from the river. It stands northeast to southwest, the southwest end buttressed with solid and well built masonry. The main walls are of adobe, plastered over. Parts of the buildings are in two stories, but everything now (1905) is in sad ruin. Though it is as solitary and deserted as San Antonio, it does not make the pathetic appeal which that venerable and dignified structure does. It is hard to say why. The photograph shows that it is not so striking a building, still there seems to be no reason why one should not feel as sadly at its desolation as one does at San Antonio. It is pathetic enough. The tiles have been taken off the roof except where they have tumbled down; others are rapidly crumbling away; some of the pillars of the corridors have fallen; weeds have grown everywhere, and instead of giving the feeling of kindly covering the desolation, they serve only to accentuate it.

"The corridors at La Purisima extended only in front of the building. The pillars are square with chamfered corners, and were evidently built of the material that happened to be readiest to hand at the moment, for some are of stone, others of burnt brick, and still others of adobe. At the time of my visit in May, 1904, eighteen pillars were still standing, and two had fallen. These pillars are about three feet square. The corridors are ten feet wide and extend the whole length of the building, which is about three hundred feet. The width, without the corridor, is about fifty feet.

"The church is at the southwest end on the southeast side. It is about eighty feet long. The windows are low and arched, but there is little left to show what were the attractions of the church, so different from any of the others. At one corner, doubtless where interested neophytes have stood looking with luminous eyes upon the movements of the officiating padre, now stands a growing tree.

"The peculiarity of La Purisima is in the architectural arrangement of the building. The church is a part,—one large room merely,—in a structure that contains many rooms. There is nothing that remains now of the wings that used to connect, and the ploughing up of the field near by has doubtless destroyed the foundations of walls, did any ever exist.

After the spoliation and abandonment of the Mission structure, the whole valley became a sort of wilderness; even the Indian rancherias gradually disappeared. The fertility of the lands, however, finally resulted in organizing the Lompoc Land Company. This association proceeded to survey a tract of land ten miles from the southern Pacific R. R. station Surf. On October 26, 1874, the survey was completed, and the lands divided into farms and town lots. At a public auction lands and town lots were disposed of to farmers and settlers who established the town of Lompoc, so named for an Indian rancheria existing there in the past.

Ere long Catholic families were attracted from the northern or San Francisco Bay District, largely through the efforts of Rev. J. B. McNally, who was in charge of the College or Seminary near Mission Santa Inés. Of the first Catholic families to settle in the town of Lompoc, were the Fabings consisting of father, mother, three sons and one daughter, Miss Flora Fabing. They arrived in 1889. The Mullinary family about the same time took up land one mile outside the town.

Gradually other homeseekers from the northern districts arrived. They were attended at the various points occasionally from the Diocesan College near Mission Santa Inés by the Rev. John B. McNally. He induced the Catholics of Lompoc to build a small church, after a plan he carried out at Santa Maria and Sisquoc also. The most notable feature of these chapels was a turret on each of the front corners. The author celebrated holy Mass in the little church of Lompoc on December 6, 1904, on occasion of a visit there, when he also measured the ruins of the first Mission.

From the year 1887, according to the *Catholic Directory*, Lompoc and other stations were attended from Mission Santa Inés. In 1910 the first resident priest arrived in the person of the Rev. John Reynolds. He was not in good health. His successor was the Rev. Charles N. Raley, who greeted the Catholics as their pastor early in 1912. The appointment was a happy one, as the sequel will demonstrate. It happened to be the 125th anniversary of the founding of Mission Purisima, the ruins of which were but three blocks away. It was also the centennial year of the founding of the second Mission across the river. Father Raley seized the opportunity to awaken the population of the city to realize the importance of having a grand celebration to commemorate both events. At a meeting of interested and public-spirited citizens, held at the new parish house on November 6, 1912, it was unanimously resolved to have a grand celebration in which all the inhabitants of the city and the surrounding country should participate.

In addition to the church services, it was decided that there should be erected a huge Cross the emblem of the Christian Faith common to all denominations, on the hillside facing the ruins of the first Mission, to perpetuate the remembrance of the celebration, and to turn the grounds round about into a park.

The Committees appointed to make the arrangements for the memorable event were as follows:

General Committee—Dr. Dimock, Chairman; Mr. McAdam, Mr. McCloskey, Mr. E. L. Mitchel, Mr. Lehman, Mr. A. G. Balaam, Rev. C. N. Raley.

Press Committee—Judge Mann, Chairman, Mr. McLean, Mr. Kirkpatrick, Mr. S. Poland, Mr. B. Grossi.

Cross Committee—Mr. Sloan, Sr., Chairman, Mr. F. Moore, Mr. Lazier.

Finance Committee—Mr. L. Kahn, Chairman, Dr. Dimock, Mr. C. D. McCabe.

FIRST CATHOLIC CHURCH AT LOMPOC.

Entertainment Committee—Mrs. McCabe, Chairman, Mrs. McLean, Mrs. F. Moore, Mr. A. G. Balaam, Mr. H. E. Harris, Mr. A. Lehman.

Reception Committee—Mayor McAdam, Chairman, Dr. Graham, Messers. C. K. Hardenbrook Sr., W. Robinson, R. Sudden, Talbott, McClure, George Pratt, A. Rudolph, Packard, W. R. Smith, J. Loynachan Graton, Bendasher, Sanor and Kalin.

The memories aroused the *Morning Press of Santa Barbara*, reported on December 6, 1912, and the sentiment inspired by the scenes that were really dramatic, on the hilltop overlooking the Lompoc valley, as the thousand people who had participated in the celebration were winding their downward course along the fresh built trail, with only the Indian chorus left to chant the benediction, made a deep impression upon all who saw and heard. For the Indians themselves, the moment was overpowering, and one of them, the aged Liberado, fell prostrate at the foot of the Cross in a faint.

Among those who took part in this observance of the 125th anniversary of the establishment of the Purisima mission, was His Excellency, Bishop Thos. J. Conaty, of the diocese of Los Angeles and Monterey. The Bishop himself blessed the large cross that is now so plainly seen from any point within the neighborhood of Lompoc, and which, by night, is outlined in electric lights. The cross stands about twenty feet high, and is made of reinforced concrete. At an elevation of 500 feet, the site is commanding.

Priests were there from many places, and the Native Sons and Daughters were represented, for they had been asked to participate, and had presented a mission bell, to mark El Camino Real, the "king's highway"—the path of the padres.

The Lompoc people were most gracious in their hospitality. From the time the visitors arrived at Surf, until the last one was escorted to the train, nothing was left undone that would contribute to the pleasure of the city's guests. The festival was civic, rather than religious; but the religious significance was not lost to sight, nor were the non-Catholics, who greatly outnumbered the Catholics, less interested or less active, in the celebration. To quote one instance—the choir of sixteen voices, which sang the Mass at the opening of the services at the cross, included but one Catholic. The celebration itself had been broached and managed by the chamber of commerce of the valley; but the ritualistic features had been left in the charge of the resident priest, Father C. N. Raley, who also shared other duties of the occasion. The public school children took part in the festivities, for it was a holiday for all Lompoc. The children marched in the procession that formed at the rectory and disbanded at the Mission site. The schools were led by the children's band, drilled by Principal A. G. Balaam. The American flag, floating over these childish heads, gave a spirit of patriotism to the parade.

This broad spirit could not but impress the visitors; and Bishop Conaty, in his address, spoke of it, with much feeling, congratulating the Lompoc people both upon their celebration and upon the liberality they had displayed.

Twelve automobiles met the Santa Barbara party at Surf. The visitors were taken into the homes of the Lompoc people, where they were entertained most hospitably during their stay.

The Santa Barbara Mission was represented by Father Zephyrin Engelhardt, O. F. M., the historian of the Franciscan Order; Father Capistran, O. F. M., and Father Aloysius, O. F. M. The Santa Barbara Jesuits were represented by Father Devlin.

Other visiting clergy included Rev. James Riordan of Long Beach; Father Buckler of Santa Inés Mission; Rev. Mestres of Monterey; Father Tiernes of Santa Maria; Father O'Riordan of San Luis Obispo, and Father McNellis of Riverside.

The Native Sons were represented by Dr. Horace Stewart and W. J. Packard, both of whom were active in preparations, being residents of the valley. Dr. Stewart and Harry Sloan conducted the procession that formed at 9:30 on H street, and marched to the hilltop where the ceremonies were held.

High Mass was sung at 10:30, with Father Buckler as celebrant, assisted by Fathers Zephyrin and Capistran. The choir was directed by W. Walley. Father Mestres, a descendent of a Spanish family that was identified with the early days of California, delivered the sermon, telling of the work of Father Serra and his successors. The Mission La Purisima was established after the death of Father Serra. His address was eloquent and inspiring.

Then followed the blessing of the cross by Bishop Conaty.

Mrs. Emma W. Lillie, past grand president of the N. D. G. W., made the address presenting the Camino Real bell which has been located at the foot of the hill upon which the cross stands. Her speech was notable, and from it may come the restoration of the Lompoc Mission.

Supervisor-elect C. K. Hardenbrook accepted the bell, thanking the Native Sons and Daughters.

State Senator Campbell of San Luis Obispo also made an eloquent address. Mayor C. R. McAdam of Lompoc and Father Raley spoke briefly, and Bishop Conaty delivered an interesting address, partly historical, and partly local on its bearing. The singing of the benediction at the foot of the cross, by the Indian chorus closed the services.

A banquet served by the ladies of Lompoc concluded the day's festivities. The committee in charge was composed of Mrs. J. D. McCabe, Mrs. May McLean and Mrs. Frank Moore. Father Raley was toastmaster; and there was much good cheer and friendly spirit. The dinner was given in Odd Fellows' hall with 250 persons present.

Among those who responded to toasts were Dr. H. C. Dimock, "The Bishop;" Mrs. Poland, president of the Alpha Literary club, "What the Alpha Club Has Done for Civic Progress in Lompoc;" Hon. Alex McLean, "Periodicals;" Mrs. Emma W. Lillie, "Our Children;" Mrs. W. W. Broughton, "Our Landmarks."

Bishop Conaty made a happy talk and a letter was read from Judge J. V. Coffey of San Francisco expressing regret that he could not be present.

Mrs. Lillie reviewed the work of the Children Agency, conducted by the N. S. G. W. and N. D. G. W.

The *Santa Barbara Independent*, on December 6, 1912, had this to say: The celebration of the anniversary of the founding of La Purisima Mission, which took place at Lompoc yesterday and was attended by hundreds of persons, marks one of the most important events in the history of Santa Barbara pioneers.

There were many distinguished persons from various parts of the state to aid in the observance of the 125th anniversary among the most prominent being Bishop Thomas Conaty of Los Angeles and Monterey, who blessed the large concrete cross which marks the place now in almost utter ruins, and which may be seen from points outside of Lompoc day or night being illuminated by electric lights. Mrs. Lillie, past grand president of the Native Daughters, also secretary of the "Children's Agency," from San Francisco, presented the El Camino Real Bell which was donated by the local parlors, and which marks the "king's highway" or the pathway of the padres.

The immense crowd that attended the ceremony yesterday was impressed by the ruins of the old historic building and the sentiment may go a long way toward building a second mission. The mixing of civic and religious sentiment made the occasion impressive and added to the feelings of hospitality always shown by the Lompoc residents on any public festival day.

The choir of 16 voices that sang the opening Mass for the cross service had but one Catholic member. The chamber of commerce of the valley had been the instrument through which the whole affair had been proposed and managed. Father C. N. Raley, the resident priest, arranged the religious program. The school children under the direction of Professor Balaam marched in a procession to the mission site, led by the children's band over which floated an immense American flag which gave a true color of patriotism to the eventful scene. These features of broad liberality were noted and emphasized by Bishop Conaty in his stirring address.

The Santa Barbara visitors were met at Surf by a long line of automobiles and every one was received and entertained in the homes of Lompoc residents who left no opportunity for comfort or pleasure unnoted for the entire visit.

The services had been well arranged and were so impressive that at the close the oldest member of the mission district, Fernando Liberado, aged 110 years, fell prostrate at the foot of the cross in a fainting condition just as the last strains of the chant in which he took an active part, died away.

The women of Lompoc furnished a sumptous banquet as an appropriate finale for the memorable occasion and several hundred sat down to the tables spread in Odd Fellows' hall. The following constituted the committee on dinner and those who responded to the toasts with Father Raley as toastmaster. Dr. H. C. Dimock, "The Bishop;" Mrs. Poland, president of the Alpha Literary club, "What the Alpha Club Has Done for Civic Progress in Lompoc;" Hon. Alex McLean, "Periodicals;" Mrs. Emma W. Lillie, "Our Children;" Mrs. W. W. Broughton, "Our Landmarks." Bishop Conaty made a happy talk and a letter was read from Judge J. V. Coffey of San Francisco expressing regret that he could not be present.

CHAPTER XII.

The Tidings, the diocesan weekly of the Diocese of Los Angeles and San Diego published a detailed report in its issue of December 13, 1912, and informed the public that a "Cross of reinforced concrete, twenty feet high has been placed on the hill overlooking the first Mission of La Purisima Concepción, standing within a few feet of where the first Cross was erected by the Mission Fathers. The site for the present Cross was given by the city trustees and will form part of a large park which will in time be developed and beautified by the city. The Cross is in a most commanding position and overlooks the entire valley, and when lighted by electricity at night the effect is most pleasing. The cross is the gift of the entire community, regardless of creed. All the citizens seemed very proud of the opportunity to commemorate the 125th anniversary of the Purisima Mission.

The dedication day was a general holiday for Lompoc, all the schools were closed, and a great number of the children were there with their parents. The procession formed at the house of Father Raley, the rector, and consisted of a long line of autos and carriages, headed by the Boys' Band, and followed by a great multitude of people who climbed the hillside and stood around the cross during the solemn ceremony. A temporary altar had been erected near the cross and Solemn Mass was celebrated, commemorative of the first Mass said by the padres after they had planted the first cross. Rev. A. Buckler, pastor of the Old Mission at Santa Inés, was celebrant; Father Zephyrin, O. F. M., and Father Capistran, O. F. M., of the Old Mission at Santa Barbara, were deacon and subdeacon, respectively, Rev. James A. Reardon, of Long Beach, was master of ceremonies. The sermon at the end of the Mass was preached by Rev. R. M. Mestres of Monterey. The music was furnished by a large volunteer choir, under the direction of Mr. W. W. Walley, which, with the exception of the organist of the Church, was composed entirely of Non-Catholics, who sang the music of the Mass with great effect.

After the Mass the Bishop in Cope and Mitre, assisted by the clergy, blessed the cross. El Camino Real bell was then blessed. This bell is the gift of the Santa Barbara Parlor of Native Daughters.

Father Raley, the rector of Lompoc, then introduced the speakers for the occasion, the first being the president of the City Council, Mr. C. O. McAdams, who gave the welcome of the city to the Bishop and the visiting clergy, and the invited guests, and in the name of the trustees accepted the Cross, pledging the city to care for it, and expressing his delight at the occasion which had brought them all together.

Senator Campbell of San Luis Obispo was then introduced, and gave the history of the foundation of the mission. He spoke of the place where they were assembled as being one of the sacred historical spots of California, made holy by the tread of the sandaled feet of those great and good Franciscan friars who, bidding adieu forever to their families, friends and country, crossed the trackless ocean in frail crafts, traversed the desert sands and penetrated the unexplored forests inhabited by savage beasts and still more savage men, in order that they might carry out the principles of their great order and be the benefactors of mankind by civilizing and Christianizing the Indians. . . . .

The next speaker was Mrs. Lillie of San Francisco, Past Grand President of the Native Daughters, who in the name of the Santa Barbara Parlor, presented the El Camino Real bell. She spoke of her delight at being present to witness the beautiful ceremony of the blessing of the cross, as well to assist at the Solemn Mass, which brought to mind so vividly the work of the early padres. She spoke very feelingly of the interest which had been created in the missions by the Native Sons and Daughters, and said it was her pleasure in their name to present the bell which would stand by the cross to remind the coming generations of the work done by the padres in the erection of buildings which even in their ruins are the pride of California.

Mrs. Lillie was followed by Mr. C. K. Hardenbrook, Supervisor of the district, who in very pleasing words, expressed his pleasure at being present, commended the work done, and graciously accepted the gift of the bell.

Bishop Conaty was then introduced, and called upon for a few words. Among other things the Bishop said:

"It is a great pleasure for me to be present at this beautiful ceremony, which has brought together all the people, regardless of religious beliefs, to take part in and witness the solemn blessing of the majestic cross which is to stand for all time as a memorial of the one planted by the padres 125 years ago, when the Franciscans first began the work of establishing the mission of La Purisima on the slopes of the hills, over-looking this beautiful valley. It is indeed inspiring to witness the magnificent demonstration of the people on this day when all seem proud to take part in the ceremony and to testify to their loving gratitude for the work done by the mission padres.

"This cross will stand as a source of inspiration to all who gaze upon it; it will serve to remind the people of this valley of the unselfishness, the apostolic life, the successful labors of as noble a band of men as ever went forth in the authority of God to preach the Cross of Christ and the lessons of Christ's redemption. The cross itself symbolizes the love of God for humanity, the unselfishness of devotion to the ideals of Christianity; it symbolizes the love of man for his fellowman; it tells of privations and sufferings endured patiently, in order that the children of the forest might be led to the knowledge of God and to civilization.

"It is a noble thing to honor men for what they are and what they have done. It is particularly gratifying when this honor is extended to men who have simply lived that other men might be benefitted, that knowledge might be extended, that morality might be established, that abandoned nations might be brought to the knowledge of the love of God for all mankind, and to the true love which men should have for one another. Among the heroes whom we honor are oftentimes men whose personal character is not worthy of imitation, but who by their deeds of bravery, or their statesmanship, have deserved recognition of a grateful people. The men whom we honor today, those brown-habited Franciscan Friars, were men whose lives were in keeping with the gospel which they preached; they were men who left their homes in far away Spain, impelled by the desire to make Christ better known and loved, and to bring the benefits of civilization into lives that knew only the things that were animal, and the habits of savages; they were men, who, after years of sanctified apostolic labor, succeeded in lifting these races into civilization, teaching them the truths of Christianity, and training them in the habits of trade and workmanship by which they were able to erect these mighty monuments of mission life, which are the wonder and admiration of the world and the pride and glory of California.

It is indeed an encouraging sight to find such a multitude gathered on this hillside today, to honor men for the deeds they did in the uplifting of humanity, and the ennobling of human character, and the leading of the wild and uncivilized races into the ways of peace and love, as well as of knowledge. It is encouraging to find that this tribute comes from many who are not followers of the Church which commissioned these Franciscan Friars, but who have reached that splendid manhood that honors the good deeds done for humanity, and who unite to proclaim the padres as men whom they love to call brethren, whose names are in benediction among them.

"I feel that it is a privilege to be here today and to take part in this beautiful ceremony; to do, here on this mountain top, what the Franciscan padres did on this very spot, 125 years ago, when they erected a cross and offered the Holy Sacrifice of the Mass as a thanksgiving to God for His kindly providence which had brought them safely to this field of their labors, and as a prayer for His blessing upon the work upon which they were about to enter.

"This cross is a memorial of their lives and their deeds; it is a beacon light to all who dwell in the valley, bidding them look up to God, to lift up their hearts to Him, and to cling closely to the cross of His redemption. It testifies to our faith in God, to our hope in His omnipotent mercy, and to our gratitude for His great love for us in giving us the inestimable blessings of Christianity.

"In the spirit of the Church of which the Franciscan Fathers were faithful members, we today bless the cross as a memorial of their lives, and we pray God, by the merits of that cross, to bless us every one, and especially to bless all who have gathered here, but in a particular manner to bless the children to whom the lesson of this day should be a constant reminder of gratitude for the deeds of great and good men who sacrificed their lives that the poorest and the lowest of God's creatures might be led into the knowledge of Christianity, and thus be brought under the influence of those divine graces by which mankind may be led into good and virtuous lives, knowing the truth and following it.

"Our congratulations then to the people of Lompoc upon this eventful day. Our grateful acknowledgment to the Mayor, the City Trustees, the Supervisor, and all who have contributed to the success of this occasion. We feel in a special sense, a debt of gratitude to the Parlor of the Native Daughters for the beautiful bell which has been blessed under the title of La Purisima. We are grateful to the committee of ladies and gentlemen who co-operated so admirably with Father Raley to make the ceremonies on this occasion memorable. A special work of praise should be given to the choir, composed, as it is of Non-Catholics, who so generously volunteered to prepare the music and sing the Mass. To God be the honor and praise! May His holy graces bring down blessings from heaven upon these people, and may this cross for generations to come, be a constant reminder of grateful recognition for the brave deeds and noble lives of the Franciscan Fathers, who established and maintained La Purisima Mission, in which and around which so many thousands of poor Indians were taught the truths of God and were trained in the ways by which to make life worth living. May the blessing of the Divine Saviour, in whose name these good men lived and died, be with us this day and all days to come."

A most pathetic incident was the gathering around the cross of a number of Indians from the Santa Inés Mission, who, under the leadership of the old Indian, Fernandito, knelt around the cross and chanted the Hymn to the Cross, which had been taught to the Indians by the padres. When the Hymn was concluded the Indians solemnly advanced to the cross and reverently kissed it. The large crowd seemed to feel the touch of the old Mission days as this simple ceremony was performed.

A banquet under the auspices of the ladies of Lompoc was given in the Odd Fellows Hall, to the Bishop, the clergy, the different committees, and the visiting Native Daughters. Mayor McAdam was also present. Rev. C. N. Raley presided, and at the close of the banquet he called upon several speakers to respond to the toasts which were proposed. Among the many who responded to toasts, Mrs. W. W. Broughton who toasted La Purisima Mission, deserves special mention. Mrs. Broughton said:

"Your Lordship, Father Raley and distinguished guests:

"I appreciate beyond words the privilege of being allowed a voice among the honored ones who have this day assisted in the beautiful ceremonial which marks another mile-stone along the King's Highway and adds another event to the history of California.

"It is indeed a privilege to have been a witness to a scene so imposing. And a thought has come to me that only those things which were inspired by high ideals in the past find permanent place in the hearts of succeeding generations. It is the glory of California that her Landmarks commemorate, not the spirit of war and violence, but rather the life of devotion to ideals, looking to God for inspiration, and finding in the needs of humanity its field of labor.

"No more fitting testimonial to the life of those early Padres could have been conceived than the placing of the cross on the hill overlooking the scene of their labor, and which has been this day consecrated to their memory, since the unselfish life leads ever along the way of love and sacrifice, of which the cross is a symbol.

"You will pardon me for saying that the quick and hearty response of our citizens to assist in this work is due in part to the fact that they are a people of ideals."

At the close, the Bishop's health was proposed, after which he responded with a short address in which he expressed his great pleasure at being able to be present and to witness the splendid unanimity of feeling and action in the erection of the beautiful cross which would stand as a lasting memorial of the good will of the community toward the memory of the early padres who built the mission. He said that such occasions were evidences of civic pride, as well as of good neighborly feeling, and it was indeed an inspiration and an encouragement to realize that all classes in the community were one, when there was question of honoring the noble lives and the deeds of the mission padres. The Bishop extended his good wishes to officials of Lompoc, the members of the various committees, and to all the citizens who had made the day such an eventful one in the history of Lompoc. He begged God's blessings on them all for what they had done, and hoped that God would keep them in that splendid neighborly feeling which should be characteristic of the best ideals of American life.

Under the heading—*The Resurrection of Lompoc*, The Monitor, diocesan weekly of San Francisco, reported as follows: under date of December 14, 1912:

Who would have thought it possible? What has happened to bring about the change? Lompoc, down in Santa Barbara

County, nine miles east of Surf on the Southern Pacific Railroad, has at last awakened to the fact that right on its southern border the city possesses a treasure which an enterprising community would have cherished long ago. The reason for the indifference was chiefly due to the bigotry of a large portion of the settlement established by people who imagined prohibition and righteousness to be synonymous terms. The few Catholics who had strayed into the district were simply lost in the crowd. Intolerance, however, cannot thrive with civilization. Civilized people think, and thinking correctly makes one considerate and broadminded. as broadminded as Almighty God's law than which there is nothing more considerate because it goes to the limit of the creature's welfare. Beyond that law freedom is no more beneficial, but destructive. So by and by the representative men and women of Lompoc also began to think, and that resulted in emancipation from the shackles of bigotry.

All well posted Californians take pride in the early history of the State, especially in the history of the twenty-one Missions which made California. The people of a pueblo or town, which can boast of squatting on or near the site of an ancient mission, regard themselves favored above other mortals, and the tourist or prospective settler is not allowed to overlook that feature. Such signally fortunate people point with special pride to the melodious name of "San" or "Santa" which the town or city retains. To even suggest a change or curtailment of the title would be considered high treason. Lompoc hitherto formed an exception. Of late this state of things, however, is otherwise. The Lompockians awoke, rubbed their eyes, and are now wide awake. They have comprehended that wide streets crossing each other at right angles in a level and fertile valley, and those running from north to south named for letters of the alphabet, are features, but not sufficiently interesting to fascinate the tourist and traveler. Such visitors inquire after the history of the place. To have been a cowpatch or sheep range, and now covered with dwellings inhabited by people who, for being "saved," presume to have the first mortgage on all that is virtuous, can hardly arrest the attention of the thoughtful visitor long enough to patronize its hotel for more than a night, if he comes for rest, recreation, and inspiration. So it has dawned upon the Lompockians that they must neglect their opportunnities no longer. Only a leader was wanted.

The leader at last arose in the person of the Rev. C. N. Raley, who in the past summer came to the valley as pastor of the Catholics scattered through the district. The time was favorable, for this year happened to be the 125th anniversary of the founding of the mission which should have given its name to the town, but which had to cede its right in favor of the Indian word Lompoc, whose meaning no one knows. With the handful of Catholics alone the celebration would have amounted to little outside the church building. Rev. Father Raley, therefore, boldly approached the most prominent citizens, and proposed a general solemnization of the event on or near the date of the founding, and thus to join the citizens of California everywhere in their efforts to interest everybody in the history of the glorious missions with a view to preserve or restore them. To his satisfaction men and women enthusiastically resolved to do their best in making the event a memorable one in the history of the town. To be sure, it could not be expected that the "saved" should contaminate themselves by associating with "sinners," but the representative people, ladies as well as gentlemen, went to work with a will, and within one month surpassed anything within the memory of the "oldest settler." Moreover, hearty good feeling was established between these liberal non-Catholics and the Catholics which of itself must be source of genuine gratification for all who participated.

The date of the establishment of the mission, December 8th, could not well be observed, so Thursday, December 5th, was selected. Little did good Father Fermin Francisco de Lasuén dream of the glorious spectacle of 1912 when one hundred and twenty-five years ago he planted the cross on the spot within four blocks of the present church, and dedicated

VARIOUS VIEWS OF MISSION PURISIMA IN ITS LAST STAGES.

the mission to God under the most beautiful title borne by any mission in California. It may justly be styled "Our Lady's Mission," "The Heavenly Queen's Mission," "Mary's Mission," for since December 8, 1787, it is known all over the coast as "La Purisima Concepción." No settlement, save that occupied by human angels, and I dare say even the "saved" would not presume to be such, is worthy of bearing the title; so it is well after all that the name of one of the mission's forty-four rancherias was substituted.

Automobiles received the Rt. Rev. Thomas J. Conaty, D. D., Bishop of Los Angeles, and various priests and interested visitors at Surf, and brought them to the town on the evening before. Next morning the parade, preceded by the public school band and the children who had considerately been given a holiday, wended its way to the foot of the mount upon which, within a stone's throw of where Fr. Lasuén stood on December 8, 1787, an immense Cross of concrete had been erected by the town's people. Back of it stood an altar. Here in the open air surrounded by several hundred spectators, most non-Catholics including the officials of the valley, High Mass was sung by Rev. Alexander Buckler of Mission Santa Inés. Two Franciscan Fathers from Santa Barbara Mission acted as deacons, while Rev. J. A. Reardon of Long Beach was master of ceremonies. His Lordship attended by Rev. A. Mestres of Monterey and Rev. B. Devlin, S. J., of Santa Barbara, assisted on an improvised throne. Rev. M. Ternes of Santa Maria and the pastor were the other priests present.

The High Mass was celebrated under rather difficult circumstances which other reverend fathers, who may contemplate similar solemnities, should by all means improve upon. With the wind blowing so that candles can not be kept burning, the Sacred Species in danger, and no shelter from the sun, the devotion of the pious Catholic must undergo severe trial. As to the non-believing witness, he will go away with anything but exalted ideas of the majesty of the Holy Sacrifice. The old padres, indeed, invariably offered holy Mass at the founding of a mission, but it was always in an "enramada," a booth or shelter of boughs, the work of a day. In this instance holy Mass should have been confined to the church only three blocks away.

Rev. Raymond Mestres after holy Mass made the address of the day to an attentive multitude. It must have been an inspiring occasion for the preacher so high above the town and so close to the ancient mission site, whose ruins are still in evidence. His Lordship then blessed the huge cross, which during the night is illuminated with electric lights, making a most beautiful spectacle as seen from the city and whole valley. A Camino Real bell, donated by the Native Daughters of Santa Barbara, I believe, was likewise blessed by the Bishop. The singing of "Holy God" closed the religious part of the celebration. Thereupon followed speeches by Mr. McAdams, the mayor, the chairman of the Board of Commerce, the past president of the Native Daughters of the State, His Lordship, and Senator Campbell of San Luis Obispo. All now descended the mountain and betook themselves to the banquet, the Bishop, the clergy and about two hundred or more ladies and gentlemen at Odd Fellow's Hall, and the general public at Foresters Hall. Here more speeches followed, all by non-Catholics. His Lordship, the Bishop, terminated the festivity with a happy talk that pleased all present. It is worthy of note that the most kindly fellowship was expressed in all the speeches, as well on the mountain as in the hall. Another evidence of the kindly feeling engendered was the choir. It consisted of the organist and fifteen or sixteen young men and young ladies, not one of whom was a Catholic. All attended the practices of the Mass with a right good will, despite the Latin which must have appeared difficult of itself, and they sang the Mass on the mount with much reverence aided by Fr. Aloysius of Santa Barbara Mission. It was a truly glorious event for the people of Lompoc, who deserve all the credit that can be lavished upon them.

It is to be hoped that the plan of restoring the Missions may be kept alive. It would be well for the people to cast their eyes on the ruins near the cross. The foundations are there still. Constructed of adobe, as it was before, it would not cost very much to reproduce it. This was the Mission occupied for twenty-five years, till the earthquake on December 21, 1812, destroyed it. The one building, whose walls are to be seen across the river, could not have been in use more than twenty years.

In the following year, November 15, 1913, the *Santa Barbara Morning Press* under the caption: *Marble Tablet Tells Story of Purisima Cross. After-Thought Develops 125th Anniversary of Last December*, contained this happy news:

"All Lompoc remembers with pleasure the Mission Memorial celebration held December 5, 1912, commemorating the 125th year of the founding of the old Purisima Mission and the erection of a large concrete cross on the summit of the hill at the head of H street, overlooking the fragmentary walls that still remain to mark the spot chosen by the old Franciscans for their first mission establishment among the Indians of this valley.

In that celebration people of all forms of religious belief joined freely and to its success contributed labor and money liberally. The great crowd that participated was actuated as a mass by a rare spirit of unanimity and concord.

"After all expenses were paid there remained in the hands of Father Raley, the priest in charge of the local parish, from the funds received for celebration purposes, the sum of $17.10. After due consideration it was decided to invest this in a marble tablet to be indented in the cross with an appropriate inscription so that the generations of the future might know the wherefore of this cross.

"A few days ago Samuel Frost, the marble man of Santa Barbara, brought up the finished tablet, a two foot square of beautiful white marble, inscribed as follows:

La Purisima Mission
Founded December 8, 1787
Destroyed December 21, 1812
Cross erected December 5, 1914
T. J. Conaty, Los Angeles, Bishop
C. N. Raley, Maryland, Pastor
Q. R. McAdams, President, City Council
Dr. Dimock, Chairman, Gen. Committee.

"The total cost of this tablet is $37.50. The difference between the fund in hand and this sum was contributed as follows:

Mr. Samuel Frost..............$10.00
Mr. Q. R. McAdams............   5.40
Dr. H. C. Dimock..............   5.40

It should be noted also that in addition to the expenses incurred in the celebration and the erection of the cross, freely met by the citizens of Lompoc, the town authorities and the electric light company have maintained a nightly illumination of the cross itself, making it a pleasing feature visible from all parts of the little city and country around.

"H street is the main one running north and south. The cross is on a high mound at its extreme southern head. It is not likely that the street will ever be utilized as such through or beyond this elevation, it being too precipitous with still rougher declivities beyond. This leaves a strip 100 feet in width which it is proposed to improve by setting out shrubbery, trees, flowers, etc., so that it may be made "a thing of beauty and a joy forever." In this work our ladies, through their associations, can materially assist, while the men do the preliminary rougher work. Many have already endorsed the idea and plans will soon be developed to carry it out.

Once more the *Santa Barbara Morning Press* had cheering news to announce. On November 13, 1914, under the heading

Planning To Rescue La Purisima Mission it informed the people that "A real old Mission in Lompoc will become an accomplished fact if the plans made by a number of citizens do not miscarry. The first steps toward restoring the old Mission La Purisima were taken last Saturday evening at a meeting held at the home of Father C. N. Raley, and it is believed that the scheme will prove feasible.

"The nucleus for the necessary funds is to be obtained from the proceeds of a lecture tour of the east to be undertaken by Father Raley this fall, his entire expenses being advanced by the Panama Pacific Exposition and the Southern Pacific company. It is also possible that the money left by the late Mary Ryan for the building of a Catholic church in Lompoc may be available for this purpose. These funds will probably total $15,000.

"According to tentative plans the old Mission in the southern part of the city is to be rebuilt as nearly as possible along the original lines, the walls being of adobe bricks, similar to those used in the first structure. A beautiful church will constitute one portion of the building.

"Probably none of the old missions have more romance connected with their names than the almost forgotten one of Mission Vieja de la Purisima Concepción. It ranks among the oldest of California's century old structures. Before its erection was entirely completed, a severe earthquake leveled it to the ground. The mission Fathers moved across the river to the site of the newer mission, carrying with them the tiling made use of in the old structure.

"Exposed to the elements the old building disintegrated rapidly until now there remains only a few ruined walls, and beneath the surface the enduring stone foundations upon which the structure was erected. Tracing these old foundations the original plan of the building may yet be seen, and it is on these foundations that the restoration is to be made."

Unfortunately Father Raley was transferred to another

parish in the south, whereupon the plan appears to have been abandoned.

No incident of note in this connection occurred until the short period of the Ku Klux Klan, which terminated so disastrously in California. "One morning the people of the town of Lompoc were horrified to see the Cross painted a brilliant red! The American League boys (to their credit may it be said) very soon returned the Cross to its natural color; and the Ladies Club of the town had the electric lights repaired. The Cross since then has been electrically illuiminated as before—a beautiful ornament for the town," as Miss Flora Fabing informs us.

APPENDIX

A

MISSION PURISIMA CONCEPCION

The most beautiful and lovely of her many titles proclaims Mary, the Mother of our Divine Saviour, absolutely sinless and stainless from the very first moment of her existence.

There ought not to be any difference of opinion on the subject, nor is there any among Catholics. Since our Mission Histories, however, circulate more among educated Non-Catholics than among the Catholic laity, it is but just that waving all theological arguments, this prerogative of the Mother of Christ be set forth clearly and briefly on the grounds of reason and common sense alone.

When the time had arrived that, in accord with the eternal decrees of the Most Holy Trinity, the Second Person of the Holy Trinity should take on human nature and human form, in order to be in everything, except sin, like unto ourselves, He became Man in the ordinary way through a woman of His choosing and making. His Almighty Power, His Infinite Wisdom and His Boundless Affection determined just what sort of a Mother this woman should be. It stands to reason that the Divine Power, Wisdom and Love would endow this woman with every perfection in the highest degree; that her intelligence would surpass the intelligence of all human creatures combined. There could be no flaw or defect in her constitution, because any imperfection would reflect upon her Divine Son. She would be an altogether wonderful creature, stainless, immaculate, the master-piece of Divine Power, Divine Wisdom, Divine Love.

Let us see what Christ—God Himself be it remembered—after the Incarnation did for His chosen Mother. He served her for thirty years at home, a model Son in loving solicitude for her before He set out on His Public Mission to mankind. Common sense will tell the thoughtful reader what the Son and mother were for each other.

Christ worked the first public miracle at her intercession; but we pass over the Public Career of Christ, and at once contemplate both Son and Mother on the heights of Calvary—Christ nailed to the Cross and His grief-stricken Mother standing loyally beneath. Christ, despite the tortures that rack His soul and body, remembers what His Mother had done for Him and what she was to Him—the most loving and solicitous of mothers. Doubtless, He had prayed the Heavenly Father for the one alleviation—that His Mother be spared the awful ordeal; but the prayer was refused. Mary must with her Divine Son drink the cup of bitter sorrows to the very dregs. Death is fast approaching. Christ realizes that His beloved Mother will be homeless. He, therefore, as His last testament bequeaths His

greatest treasure on earth to His beloved disciple John. "Woman, behold
thy son." Then He turns to the disciple; "Son, behold thy Mother." And
from that hour John took the Mother of his Divine Master to his own.—
    We have reached for millions upon millions of souls the parting of the
ways which separation has continued to this day. It was and is the uni-

STELLA MATUTINA

versal belief of Christ's true followers. that John here represented the
faithful of all times. These true believers in turn were quick to see that
Mary was given charge of the faithful in the capacity of Mother for all
time to come. They have the conviction that, since Mary had such influence with her Son on earth, in her heavenly glory she must be all power-

ful to secure for her adopted sons and daughters whatever they might ask in prosperity or adversity. Hence their undying affection for the Mother of their Divine Saviour. In short, they feel they are not orphans, but in the safe-keeping of a mighty and sympathetic Mother.

Christ Himself loves them for their loyalty to His Mother, as may be gathered from their unanimity in the Christian Faith for which millions have suffered the death of martyrs, and which has animated other millions to strive after Christian perfection as virgins consecrated to the Spouse of virgins, Christ Himself.

How different the story of those who at any time have separated from the Fold and have travelled other roads. They call themselves Christian; but Christ manifestly knows them not. He offered to entrust to His Mother the care of all that believe in Him. Sad to say, they declined her protection. One should think that the feminine portion of these wanderers at least, would feel proud that one of their sex, not a man, is exalted in heaven above all human and angelic creatures. Instead, the mere name of Mary, the Mother of Christ, as we have observed repeatedly, produces a frosty silence, withering stare, or studied indifference at best. What a pity! What has Mary done to them? Can they imagine that such disdain for His Mother will be agreeable to her Divine Son? What would every mother's son of us do in such circumstances?

The term Mother-of-God, especially, arouses disgust among those not of the Faith. God was long before her, they insist, and therefore Mary cannot be so styled. For the same reason any woman might not call herself the mother of John or of Lucy, because she did not bear John or Lucy but only the body of John or Lucy, since the soul came from Almighty God. However, with the true believers in Christ the question has been settled for all time to come by the General Council of Ephesus held in 431, just fifteen hundred years ago. Amid the acclamation and the rejoicing of the people the Council declared Mary to be truly the Mother of God— *Theotókos*.

Now, what are the effects of the sectarian attitude regarding Mary? The same that occurred in past centuries. Every sect in the past as in the present time possessed this distinctive feature: hostility to Mary, the Mother of the Saviour. All fared the same way: steady disintegration, rapid dissolution, total disappearance. What else could be expected? The Lord ignored and disowned them in the past and He is ignoring and disowning them in our day for ignoring and disowning His Mother. To all the clamors of such would-be-Christians, Christ has but one answer:— *Love Me, Love My Mother.*

Accordingly, the devotion of the faithful for the Mother of their Divine Saviour, everywhere and at all times, assumed an entirely childlike character, and resulted in applying to Mary all sorts of endearing names and titles.

128 Missions and Missionaries of California

Not only individuals, but whole nations, cities, organizations, etc., chose the Mother of Jesus as their Patroness, Protectress, and chief Intercessor with her Divine Son. For instance, to remain at home, the Bishops, of the United States assembled for the Sixth Provincial Council at Baltimore in 1846, petitioned the Holy Father to ratify their choice of the Blessed Virgin Mary, as Patron of the country, under the title, "Immaculate Conception." It so happened that, on founding the Mission in Lompoc Valley, nearly seventy years previously, the Franciscan Fathers placed their Indian flock and the church in the protection of the same Virgin Mother under the same title of Immaculate Conception, as the reader will find in the first chapter of this little volume, although this Mission was better known as *Purisima Concepcion*, which with the Spaniards meant the same thing,— *Esto es, de su Concepcion Inmaculada.*

Another instance is the Empire of the Rising Sun, Japan, The Catholic Hierarchy of that country declared the Mother of Jesus to be the Patron of that Land under the title "Stella Matutina" (Morning Star).

B

RANCHERIAS ATTACHED TO MISSION PURISIMA CONCEPCION
(According to the Padron.)

Ajuaps, or *La Larga*	Lououato del Tular
Aguam	Miquiui or Dos Pueblos
Atajes	Nahucu, or Graciosa Nueva
Auajue	Nimquelquel
Calauasa	Nipomo
Coouseup	Nocto
Cuiam	Nilaluy
Echiuchiu	Nomgio, or Gaviota
Ejpe	Niacla
Esgeliulimu	Sahpili, or Graciosa Vieja
Esniceue	Sacciol, or Los Alamos
Esqueue	Silegini
Estep,—San Antonio de	Silimastus, or La Espada
Estavit, or Bulito	Sisolop, or El Cojo
Guaslaic	Silimi
Hachi, or La Quemada	Sipuc
Hujuali	Sisuou
Itiase	Sajuchu, or Santa Rosa
Itxemen	Toan
Jalama	Tejas, or Santa Anita
Jonjonata	(Jalama)
Lacaiamu	Tajauchu, or Santa Rosa
Liseauato	Uasna
Lompoc	Uenejel
Lospe	

C

SPIRITUAL RESULTS AT MISSION PURISIMA CONCEPCION.—1788-1846.

Year	Baptisms Ind.	Wh.	Marriages Ind.	Wh.	Deaths Ind.	Wh.	Indians M.	F.	Total Exist	Confirmation	Communions	Viaticum	Confirmations
1787..													
1788..	95		25						95				
1789..	162		38		7				151				
1790..	308		63		25				278				263
1791..	488		97		51				434				199
1792..	598		117		86				510				
1793..	663		122		113				546				298
1794..	804		169		138				656				129
1795..	935		206		181				743				
1796..	997		222		226		383	373	756				
1797..	1132		257		266				842				
1798..	1229		285		307		448	472	920				
1799..	1301		299		364				937				
1800..	1380	3	320		420	1	460	501	961				
1801..	1472		333		516				956				
1802..	1581		356		557	1	457	571	1028				
1803..	2033		473		610				1436				
1804..	2214	2	534		707		685	835	1520				
1805..	2328	1	569		800								
1806..	2360	2	627		1020		533	633	1166				
1807..	2394		640		1108				1124				
1808..	2425	2	656		1170	2	502	582	1084				
1809..	2453		669		1243				1031				
1810..	2495		683		1312		500	520	1020				
1811..	2534	2	689		1399		480	498	978				
1812..	2595	2	725		1443		489	510	999	455	110		
1813..	2680	1	750		1518	1	507	497	1010	200	80	6	
1814..	2729	4	772		1586		496	486	982	578	88	20	
1815..	2846	2	818	1	1675		510	509	1019	600	177	21	
1816..	2920	2	840		1755		515	503	1018	597	173	17	
1817..	2955	1	857		1846		486	472	958	840	163	6	
1818..	2991	1	872		1915		481	456	937	570	63	12	
1819..	3019	4	877		1980	1	468	420	888	112	60	8	
1820..	3046		888		2054		452	388	840	568	96	4	
1821..	3075	2	912		2112	1	435	373	808	581	125	7	
1822..	3099		918	1	2172	1	413	351	764	481	315	8	
1823..	3121	4	931	2	2243		496	326	722	519	322	6	
1824..	3138	2	943		2324	4	366	296	662				
1825..	3163		956		2370	2390	300	232	532	100	30		
1826..	3173	1	968		2446	1	234	287	521	100	40	6	
1827..	3183	1	974		2486	1	201	270	471	70	31	5	
1828..	3199	1	996		2527	1	193	252	445	90	41	3	
1829..	3213		1004		2561		170	236	406				
1830..	3224		1010		2563		179	234	413	115	30		
1831..	3244		1011		2549	1	180	224	404	50	30	4	
1832..	3255		1020		2633		227	145	372				
1833..	3266		1034		2658								
1834..	3325		1043		2688								
1835..	3334		1045		2732								
1836..	3342		1053		2760								
1837..	3347		1054		2781								
1838..	3350		1060		2905								
1839..	3357		1064		2821								
1840..	3361		1065		2839								
1841..	3364		1076		2860								
1842..	3371		1086		2880								
1843..	3375		1090		2894								
1844..	3377		1091		2964								23
1845..	3381	40	1092	4	2972								712
1846..	3386		1094			16							

MATERIAL RESULTS AT MISSION PURISIMA CONCEPCION, AGRICULTURAL RESULTS.—1788 to 1832.

Year	Wheat		Barley.		Corn		Beans		Peas		Total		
	Plt.	Hrv.	Plt.	Hrv.	Plt.	Hrv	Plt.	Hrv.	Plt.	Hrv.	Plt.	Hrv.	Bushels
1788	.....	......	....	.....	1	144	1	7	....	.....	2	151	255
1789	.....	......	....	.....									
1790	25	530	11	16	3	521	4	70	2	2	35	1139	1898
1791	76	800	....	.....	4	653	3!	131	.2	2	111	1584	2640
1792	61	602	....	.....	4	891	4	90	....	.....	69	1583	2633
1793	55	1102	....	.....	6	200	3	80	....	.....	64	1382	2303
1794	68	1254	....	.....	3	549	3	38	....	.....	74	1841	3068
1795	96	308	....	.....	4	503	2	7	....	.....	102	818	1363
1796	75	1250	....	.....	2	65	2	28	.1	1	79	1344	2240
1797	65	1700	....	.....	2	.....	2	11	.3	1	69	1712	2853
1798	92	1900	....	.....	5	38	2	24	.2	2	95	2002	3336
1799	92	2500	1	70	1	15	2	70	.2	8	96	2663	4438
1800	69	1200	....	.....	1	150	1	85	....	.....	71	1435	2392
1801	165	1600	12	8	1	130	1	38	.2	10	168	1786	2977
1802	96	1000	.2	5	1	160	1	38	.1	1	98	1194	1990
1803	161	500	....	.....	1	125	3	65	....	.....	165	690	1150
1804	230	3000	....	.....	3	130	3	80	....	.....	236	3210	5350
1806	300	1200	10	50	3	200	8	34	....	.....	321	1484	2473
1807	400	1000	10	50	3	400	8	35	....	.....	421	1485	2475
1808	177	2000	3	10	5	450	4	25	....	.....	189	2495	4142
1809	176	1800	6	60	6	600	5	66	3	45	196	2571	4285
1810	200	3000	13	360	4	506	4	60	3	55	224	3981	6635
1811	180	3000	25	800	4	450	4	115	11	510	224	4875	8125
1812	150	3000	....	.....	1	50	3	27	....	.....	154	3077	5128
1813	150	3600	100	2000	7	2000	2	26	8	380	267	8006	13343
1814	100	1000	....	.....	6	2000	8	200	7	270	121	3470	5783
1815	180	2000	3	50	6	400	4	80	12	350	205	2880	4800
1816	123	2500	18	600	8	1000	5	120	17	1044	171	7264	8773
1817	157	2800	39	500	8	1000	6	200	22	586	232	5086	8476
1818	250	3000	12	200	2	200	2	60	19	1031	285	4491	7485
1819	180	2900	6	200	6	900	6	125	13	500	211	4625	7708
1820	208	2435	....	.....	4	.....	7	54	3	37	222	2526	4210
1821	240	4000	13	334	6	400	11	300	12	294	282	5328	8880
1822	150	1587	....	.....	7	900	4	106	1	25	162	2618	4363
1823	150	1500	....	.....	4	200	2	15	1	25	157	1740	2900
1824	.....	......	....	.....	....	.....	....	.....	....	.....	119	1221	2035
1825	.....	......	....	.....	....	.....	....	.....	....	.....	103	2316	3860
1826	150	2000	....	.....	4	80	4	60	4	13	162	2153	3588
1827	120	2000	12	60	4	800	6	70	4	9	146	2839	3899
1828	102	1000	15	58	7	200	4	82	2	35	130	1375	2292
1829	90	300	10	80	4	400	3	89	2	33	109	902	1503
1831	70	700	14	56	4	100	3	20	1	17	92	893	1488
1830	.....	......	....	.....	....	.....	....	.....	....	.....	72	967	1612
1832	.....	......	....	.....	....	.....	....	.....	....	.....	71	669	1115
1833	.....	......	....	.....	....	.....	....	.....	....	.....			
1834	.....	613	....	302	....	150	....	115	....	48	....	1228	2047

Total Bushels................172,261

Adding the average of 4005 bushels a year for the three missing years, we shall get a total product of all kinds of grain of **189,276** bushels in forty-six years.

MATERIAL RESULTS AT MISSION PURISIMA CONCEPCION—LIVESTOCK
1787 to 1834.

Year	Cattle	Sheep	Goats	Pigs	Horses	Mules	Total
1787	83	166	99	2	46	12	408
1788	99	188	134		44	14	479
1789	169						
1790	270	464	267		74	14	988
1791	232	603	292	11	87	19	1244
1792	311	626		24	94	20	1075
1793	380	1142		40	139	25	1726
1794	456	1587		41	148	23	2255
1795	607	1503			143	27	2280
1796	700	2200		12	175	32	3119
1797	900	3300		24	186	36	4446
1798	1016	3700		18	204	36	4974
1799	1400	4000		19	214	40	5673
1800	1600	4000			250	36	5886
1801	2000	4300		26	268	50	6644
1802	2640	5400		25	326	44	8435
1803	3230	5400		14	306	66	9016
1804	3736	4967		15	338	46	9102
1805							
1806	5000	6000		30	590	50	11640
1807	5000	7000		30	700	80	12810
1808	7000	10000		60	775	90	17925
1809	10000	11000		66	1300	95	22461
1810	8000	10000		42	1100	106	19248
1811	7000	9000		40	1080	100	17220
1812	4000	12000		60	1150	100	17310
1813	5000	12000		60	1100	156	18376
1814	8000	12000		60	1160	160	21389
1815	8000	12000		120	1110	212	21442
1816	8500	11000		160	1217	190	20067
1817	8500	11500		150	1300	225	21675
1818	9000	12000		100	1300	230	22630
1819	9000	12000		100	1010	225	22335
1820	9500	12600		86	1305	238	23729
1821	11000	11000		100	1354	252	23746
1822	10000	11000	46	104	1367	257	21774
1823	10500	10000	33	110	1445	330	22418
1824	10000	6000	30	100	1200	300	17630
1825	6000	8365	27	124	1230	300	16046
1826	10100	6150	31	100	1200	300	17881
1827	10202	9000	24	125	1105	300	20756
1828	10200	9000	30	100	1000	150	20480
1829	8000	6000	30	30	1000	146	15206
1830	7000	6000	20	50	1000	155	14225
1831	10500	7000	30	62	1000	160	18752
1832	9200	3500	20	65	1000	200	13985
1833							
1834	6200	6458	16	40	1200	70	14042

INDEX

A

Abella, Fr. Ramon, O. F. M., 84
Account Book, 46
Achup, Indian God, 22
Aguilar, Francis X., 29
Alabado, Hymn, 80
Alemany, Most Rev. José Sadoc, O. P., D. D., 66, 72, 74
Algsacupi, Site of, 6; Rancho of, 32, 35, 38
Aloysius, Fr., O. F. M., 105
Alvarado, J. B., 30
Alvisio, Corporal Nicolas, 52
Ambris, Rev. Doroteo, 86
American League Boys, 124
Amuu, Plain of, 35
Andrés, José, Indian Executed, 53
Anthony, St., Wonderworker, 45
Antonio, Indian Executed, 53
Apache, 13
Aráncel, (Pricelist), 16
Arce, Sergeant José M., 48
Arenaza, Fr. Pasqual, O. F. M., 89
Arguello, Gov. José 46; Gov. (temporory) Luis, 57
Arrillaga, Gov. José Joaquin, 31, 34
Arroita, Jr. José (Francisco), O. F. M., 7, 10, 81, 89
Arroyo, Fr., see Cuesta
Arroyo Seco, 19
Auto-de-Visita, 7, 93
Avila, Bruno, 47

B

Balaam, Mr. A. G., 102, 105
Baltasar, Indian Executed, 53
Bancroft, Herbert H, Historian, 50, 53, 58
Baptisms, Book of, 6; At First Site, 36; Interesting Note of, 82; Remarkable Number of, 83; Total Number of, 58
Bendasher, Mr., 104
Benedict XIV, Pope, 27
Benito, Indian Ringleader, 53
Bernabe, Indian Ringleader, 53
Bonaventure, St., Statue of, 45
Borica, Gov. Diego, 9, 10, 12, 90

Boscana, Fr. Geronimo, O. F. M., 19, 22, 37, 97
Botello, Narciso, Assemblyman, 64
Boussier, Rev. Theodosius, C. SS. CC., 88
Briones, Señora Guadalupe, Infirmarian, 41
Broughton, Mrs. W. W., 114
Buckler, Rev. Alexander, 105
Burial Register, Title Page of, 86; Interesting Note in, 87; Last Entry in, 88; Total Number in, 58

C

Cabot, Fr. Juan, O. F. M., 21, 97
California and the Missions, Glimpses of, 99
Calzada, Fr. José Antonio, O. F. M., 8, 10, 21, 37, 81
Camino Real, 32, 104
Campbell, State Senator, 106
Capistran, Fr.,Damek, O. F. M., 105
Carlos III, King of Spain, 6
Carrillo, Sergeant Anastasio, 50; Assemblyman Carlos, 64; Commissioner Domingo, 56; Joaquin, 57; Lieut. Raimundo, 30
Casimiro, Indian Interpreter, 82
Castro, Soldier, 48
Catholic Directory, 102
Cavaller, Fr. José, O. F. M., 95
Celebration Extraordinary, 102
Cipriano, Indian Killed, 50
Clement XI, Pope, 27
Coffey, Judge J. V., 106
Colima, Simón, 50
Colton, Rev. Walter, Protestant Minister, 60; Statements of, 61
Comanche, 13
Conaty, Most Rev. Thomas J., 104
Confessionario, 22
Confirmations, Register of, 79; Last, 81
Congress, Act of, 66
Converts, Yearly Average of, 79
Cordero, Miguel of Santa Inés, 61

L

La Graciosa, Cuesta de, 41, 51
Lalsacupi, Rancho of, 26
Larga, Thomas de la, 25; Rancho de la, 42
Lasuén, Fr. Fermin de, O. F. M., Presidente of Missions, 5, 8, 12, 18, 80, 86, 102
Lazier, Mr., 102
Lehman, Mr. A., 102, 104
Librado, Aged Indian, 104
Lillie, Mrs. Emma W., 106
Lipan, Indian Dialect, 13
Lippincott, L. K., 73
Literas Edificantes, 21
Lompoc, 18; Valley of, 39; Ladies Club of, 124; Land Company of, 101; Resurrection of, 115
Lopez, Map of, 35
Loreto, Mansisidor de, 50
Los Angeles, 50
Los Alamos, Rancho of, 57; Mission of, 87
Los Berros, 32; Locality of, 34
Lugo, Santiego, 56

M

Maitorena, Ensign Joaquin, 30
Malo, Ramon, 64
Mann, Judge, 102
Marble Tablet, Inscription of, 122
Mariano, Indian Ringleader, 53
Marquez, Agustin, Soldier, 16
Marriage Register, 79; Title Page of, 88; Total Number in, 58
Martiarena, Fr. Josepf, O. F. M., 90
Martin, Fr. Juan, O. F. M., 90
Martinez, Fr. Pedro Adriano, O. F. M., 97
Matisaquit, First Indian Baptized, 7
Maytoreno, Ensign, 47
McAdam, Mayor, 104
McCabe, Mr. C. D., 102; Mrs., 104
McCloskey, Mr. 102
McClure, 104
McLean, Mr., 102; Mrs., 104
McNally, Rev. J. B., 101
McNellis, Rev., 105
Mestres, Rev., 105
Micheltorena, Gov. Manuel, 62; Decree of, 62; Exiled, 63

Miguel, Fr. José de, O. F. M., 37, 96
Mission Fund, 30
Missions, Sold at Auction, 64
Mitchel, Mr. E. L., 102
Mofras, Duflot de, Traveller, 60
Monitor, The, 115
Monjério, 42
Moore, Mr. F., 102; Mrs. F., 104
Mora, Most Rev. Francis, 73, 77
Moreno, Fr. Juan, O. F. M., 58, 62, 64
Morgan, Rev. John, 98
Morning Press, The Santa Barbara, 104
Morris, Rev. Thomas B., 98
Mullinary, Family of, 101

N

Native, Daughters of California, 104; Sons of California, 104
Neuia, Indian Chief, 82
Neve, Gov. Felipe de, 3

O

Observance of Mission's 125th Anniversary, 104
O'Connell, Rev. Eugene, 86
Oliva, Fr. Vincente, O. F. M., 45, 97
Orámas, Fr. Cristóbal, O. F. M., 8, 81, 89
Ordáz, Fr. Blas, O. F. M., 50
O'Riordan, Rev., 105
Ortega, Family of, 26; Eugenio, 59; Francisco, 30; Juan, 30
O'Shea, Rev. Timothy, 98
Oso Flaco, 25, 51
Otomite, Indian Dialect, 13

P

Pacheco, Don Francisco, 52
Pacifico, Indian Executed, 53
Packard, Mr. W. J., 105
Pacomio, Indian Ringleader, 53
Padron, 79
Pala, Asisténcia, 94
Panella, Fr. Joseph, O. F. M., 96
Pangua, Fr. Thomas de, O. F. M., 90; Fr. Francisco, O. F. M., 3
Pasados por las Armas, 53
Patentes, Libro de, 41
Paterna, Fr. Antonio, O. F. M., 89
Pathetic Incident, 114

LAUS DEO

Distance from Mission Santa Barbara—20 leagues

Distance to Mission Santa Inés—8 leagues

The Missions of California

(Correct dates of their founding)

———

San Diego de Alcala, July 16, 1769.

San Carlos Borromeo, or Carmelo, June 3, 1770.

San Antonio de Padua, July 14, 1771.

San Gabriel, Arcangel, September 8, 1771.

San Luis Obispo, September 1, 1772.

San Francisco de Asis, or Dolores, June 29, 1776.

San Juan Capistrano, November 1, 1776.

Santa Clara de Asis, January 12, 1777.

San Buenaventura, March 31, 1782.

Santa Barbara, December 4, 1786.

La Purisima Concepcion, December2, 1787.

Santa Cruz, August 28, 1791.

La Soledad, October 9, 1791.

San José, June 11, 1797.

San Juan Bautista, June 24, 1797.

San Miguel, Arcangel, July 25, 1797.

San Fernando Rey, September 8, 1797.

San Luis Rey, June 13, 1798.

Santa Inés, September 17, 1804.

San Rafael, Arcangel, December 14, 1817.

San Francisco Solano, July 4, 1823.

FATHER ENGELHARDT'S HISTORICAL WORKS

ILLUSTRATED

The Franciscans in California. Edition Exhausted.

The Franciscans in Arizona. Edition Exhausted.

The Holy Man of Santa Clara. Edition Exhausted.

Vida del P. Magín Catalá, O. F. M., Spanish. Cloth $1.00

The Missions and Missionaries of California, Vol. I. Eecond Edition, 810 pages. Bound in cloth $4.00

The Missions and Missionaries of California. Vol. II. Second Edition, Cloth. 730 pages $4.00

The Missions and Missionaries of California. Vol. III. Cloth. 680 pages $4.00

The Missions and Missionaries of California. Vol. IV. Cloth. 832 pages $4.00

Index for volumes ii-iv. Cloth. 190 pages $1.50

Above set of five books by mail or express $15.00

Mission San Diego. The Mother of the Missions. Cloth. 372 pages..$2.50

Mission San Luis Rey. The King of the Missions. Cloth. 275 pages..$2.00

Mission San Juan Capistrano. The Jewel of the Missions. Cloth 270 pages $2.00

Mission San Gabriel. The Pride of the Missions. Cloth. 370 pages..$2.00

Mission San Fernando. The Mission of the Valley. Cloth. 170 pages $1.50

Mission Santa Barbara. The Queen of the Missions. Cloth. 488 pages $3.00

Mission San Francisco, or Mission Dolores. Cloth. 450 pages........$2.50

Mission San Miguel, Mission San Antonio, Mission Soledad, the three in one volume. Cloth. 350 pages..$2.50

Mission San Buenaventura. The Mission by the Sea. Cloth............$1.75

Mission San Juan Bautista, A School of Church Music................$1.50